Martial Arts America

Martial Arts America

A Western Approach to Eastern Arts

Bob Orlando

Frog, Ltd.
Berkeley, California

Published by Frog, Ltd.

Frog, Ltd. books are distributed by
North Atlantic Books
P.O. Box 12327
Berkeley, California 94712

Cover and Illustrations by Michael Dolcé
Photographs by Roy A. Sorenson
Cover and book design by Catherine E. Campaigne

Printed in the United States of America by Printer

Library of Congress Cataloging-in-Publication Data
Orlando, Bob.
    Martial arts America : a Western approach to Eastern arts / Bob Orlando.
        p.   cm.
    Includes bibliographical references and index.
    ISBN 1-883319-67-6
    1. Martial arts—Study and teaching—United States.   I. Title.
GV1100.A2075   1998
796.8—dc21   97-38087
                                                                CIP

2   3   4   5   6   7   8   9   /   02   01   00   99   98

To Edmund K. Parker

Although a long-time admirer of Ed Parker, I have never been a student of his or his AMERICAN KENPO KARATE. Few, however, have influenced my martial art thinking as much as he. He is gone now, and the martial art community is poorer for it. I can only hope that those who continue to carry his flame do so in the same spirit as he.

Table of Contents

Foreword

by Robert Pickett, Chong Shin Kwan

The martial arts industry in this country is enjoying a period of tremendous popularity. People of all ages—concerned by rapidly increasing rates of violence and abuse, or desirous of feelings of confidence and control—have turned to the fighting arts by the thousands. The martial arts have never been so lucrative for so many.

However, the more potential for profit, the more closely a product and its sales force should be scrutinized. Too often people pursue a program of martial art instruction without any investigation into its purpose, history, or philosophies. Also, students can easily be taken advantage of due to the way martial arts are typically taught.

For decades, Americans have been told that to gain the full benefit from their study of the martial arts, they must submit to Eastern teaching methods. In general, these methods require that students take the instructor's word as undeniable fact. There is no acceptable format in which students may question technique or doctrine. American students, desperate to grasp the intricacies of Asian martial arts, have uncharacteristically acquiesced.

Many students spend years training, progress in rank, and even accept teaching positions without doing that for which Americans are famous (or infamous)—questioning authority. They fail to ask two familiar American questions: "Why?" and "Can you prove it?"

In the chapters that follow, Bob Orlando asks those questions and many more. He first puts the martial arts into historical, cultural, and practical perspective. Then he explores the major components of martial art training and provides alternatives to the traditional teaching methods. With nearly three decades of experience in a wide variety of styles, Mr. Orlando is well qualified for the task. His investigative ability as a computer systems analyst and his extensive study of spiritual and religious matters allow for an intellectual approach to some very emotional subjects.

Although this book is intended specifically for the self-defense-oriented martial artist, students regardless of goal or level of expertise, will benefit from its consideration and discussion of Mr. Orlando's ideas. In addition, the material should serve as a source of self-analysis and reflection for instructors and leaders. Even those who disagree with the author's conclusions will surely admit the importance of his questions.

Acknowledgments

As I consider the help I have received in writing this book, several people come to mind as having contributed, in a special way, to its existence. First and foremost is my wife of more than thirty-one years. I mention the years because at the time we were married, I was not seriously involved in the martial arts. When she accepted my marriage proposal, martial art study and training were not part of the deal. Many have started down the martial way only to be forced off the road because their spouses could not understand the commitment such a journey demands. Fortunately for me, God gave me a wife who not only understands, but willingly supports my efforts. Without her, neither my martial skill nor publishing successes would be possible.

When I think of those who have been the most instrumental in my growth as a martial artist I think of men like Al Dacascos. His instruction in my early years influences my training and study to this day. I also think of Dr. John Cochran; the only kenpo instructor I know with a Ph.D. in Economics. John taught me the real meaning of courage. Facing what looked to be overwhelming physical limitations, John inspired me to continue training. It was from him that I received my first degree black belt.

Ron Carlson built on Cochran's work and extensively directed and sharpened my self-defense skills. In the Taoist tradition of martial art training, one progresses from hsing-I (having developed the necessary physical strength and mental toughness), through pa kua (where the practitioner reaches a high level of technical competence), and finally to t'ai chi (where the result becomes a supreme blend of strength, technique, and mental balance that flows without conscious effort). In my own way a similar path brought me to my current instructor, Mr. Willem de Thouars.

Although his students address him as "Uncle," this man allows me to call him "Bill" (that does not mean that I am his equal). In my time with him, Bill has shared much more with me than just his native arts of *kuntao* and *pentjak silat*; he has also given me his very heart and soul. I call him "Bill," but in my heart, he is family—a real Dutch "Uncle." Willem de Thouars epitomizes the martial art "master" because he refers to everyone but himself as such. He often says that this individual or that is a "master in his own art." He even extends that compliment to those that have abused his friendship. For himself, however, he says only that he has some skills. (In his culture, martial artists trained to survive—not for rank.)

Besides my teachers and training partners, four individuals were especially instrumental in the development of this work: Mr. Stewart Lauper, Mr. Barry Benedict, Mr. Edward "Dan" Daniels, and Ms. Kathy Fink.

Stewart Lauper is, pound-for-pound, the toughest, hardest-hitting man I know. He is also one of the most encouraging and generous individuals I have ever been fortunate enough to know. Stewart has been a constant source of encouragement and ideas in my writing and my training.

Barry Benedict is the gentleman who introduced me to his instructor, Ed Parker. Aside from Parker's writings, many of the insights I have into that great martial artist come from Barry. Barry's skill is formidable and a testimony to the effectiveness of Ed Parker's art, but in my mind, Barry's love of the art and his willingness to help others succeed in their martial walk (even those taking a different path) are his clearest reflections of Ed Parker.

Dan Daniels is a close personal friend and one of my best students. Despite this, he is one from whom I get little respect, for Dan is a brutal editor. He is also the one man who knows my writing style and my feelings about the art better than anyone. Like myself, Dan is a "full-time" martial artist. Although his occupation keeps him on the road a good deal, he always finds time to do a number on my writing. I am fortunate that he is my friend, for if he were an enemy, his cutting and slashing would be worse than murder. As a friend, Dan is one of the first I call on for review and reality check—in my writing and in my art.

Although a cliché, "last but not least" is especially true here. Kathy Fink is a professional associate with whom I have worked many years. Although never formally involved in the martial arts, her nonmartial but professional point of view was invaluable. Moreover, saying that she was *very instrumental* in providing the feminine perspective would be the grossest understatement.

Introduction

When a skill or sport is transferred to another country, that country should replace the foreign training methods with methods reflecting and exploiting its own characteristics, needs, and virtues.

—G. R. Gleeson, 1967
Judo for the West

Asian fighting and martial arts have been practiced in the United States for more than 100 years. However, for more than half of that time, they were taught and practiced almost exclusively in those emigrant communities that brought them here. After World War II, all of this changed. On returning from duty in the Far East, American servicemen began sharing what they were privileged to learn, and the stories they told enthralled us.

Soon after, Asian masters began touring the country, performing exhibitions and demonstrating their martial prowess. They broke stacks of boards, bricks, and even bull's horns, and we were impressed. In the last forty years, instructors of Asian arts have flooded our shores and, today, martial art schools are practically everywhere—from Los Angeles to New York to La Junta, Colorado. But a martial art is like a garden, and periodically, it must be weeded.

The American garden has become overgrown with weeds and it must, once again, be weeded and cultivated. I say "once again" because this is not the first time this process has been attempted. Many culturally American martial art instructors and teachers have questioned the training methods, practices, and traditions of their arts. However, of the voices asking *why,* only a few were influential enough to be heard above the din of opposition. Two *effectual* voices in America's journey down Asia's martial way—two modern martial art pioneers—are the late Ed Parker and Bruce Lee.

Bruce Lee

BRUCE LEE, 1940–1973

When Lee made his mark in martial art history, he was—relative to the masters of his time—a young man. However, what he lacked in experience he more than made up for in desire, energy, raw physical talent, and—most importantly—his inquisitive and analytical mind. His confidence in his quest and in the truth behind his ideas still runs against the grain of many in the established martial art community, but the impact of his message on American martial arts cannot be overstated. More than two decades after his seemingly premature death, Lee remains as controversial as ever. However, his popularity, even now, attests to his influence and the validity of his ideas.

Ed Parker

Chronologically, Parker's pioneering effort parallels Lee's. His method, however, was different. Lee (almost as if he knew his time was short) came across as confrontational to the point of antagonism. Parker also challenged the status quo, but his approach was less explosive and more calculated—like

COURTESY OF LELANI PARKER, 1995

EDMUND K. PARKER, 1931–1990

that of a general working a well-planned and perfectly executed campaign strategy. Despite his less antagonistic approach, Parker also faced considerable opposition and hostility for daring to go against "tradition." However, his success in developing an effective system of self-defense, coupled with the depth of his world-wide organization, stands as testimony to the fact that many, many others had (and still have) similar concerns about the state of martial arts as practiced in the West.

Despite the best efforts of modern martial art giants like Parker and Lee, the past half-century has seen the American martial art garden become overgrown with weeds—weeds that obscure the purpose, value, and worth of martial art study and training. G. R. Gleeson, national coach to the British Judo Association, said it best when he described a similar situation that occurred in judo. He said,

> Judo, because it had its origin in a period of time which was virtually feudalistic, has become somewhat contaminated with an obfuscatory aura of feudalistic mumbo-jumbo, with the result that subsequent teachers, for various reasons, have insisted on treating judo as a feudalistic, esoteric "art" and have taught it as such, mistaking the original or early environmental manifestations of the training as the essence of the skill (Gleeson 1967, 13).

The same problem occurs today in the United States. Too many take the cultural trappings, the outward manifestations of their arts, and esteem them as the very essence of those arts. Clearly, it is time to weed the garden.

The Central Truth

The central truth running through these pages is that *philosophies and methods of instruction must match the culture of those being instructed.* This truth looms even larger when the gulf between the cultures involved is measured in time as well as physical distance. Recognizing this truth—and acting on it—is the focus of this book.

My purpose in the following chapters is to examine Eastern martial art training practices and philosophies, consider their origins, and appraise their relevance to the American student. In this examination there are no sacred cows. No topic is taboo. Martial art traditions, rituals, philosophies, training practices, religious influences, and even gender issues are all examined in depth. With each topic, changes—some of them radical; all of them practical—are suggested that can significantly improve the process of sharing Eastern martial arts with Western-thinking Americans.

Martial Arts America is intended primarily for the individual whose main interest in martial art study and training is effective self-defense. Such a motivation does not preclude investigation, study, assimilation, or integration of the other areas of interest offered by Eastern martial arts, but it does draw a line in the sand.

Martial Arts America can not cover every issue. However, the issues it does address should serve to challenge every practitioner—student and teacher, traditional and nontraditional, novice and expert—to think critically about every part of what he or she is learning and teaching. Whether you agree or disagree with the ideas and conclusions presented here is not nearly as important as your commitment to honestly consider the issues and logically formulate your own *reasoned* position.

For some, the questions raised within these pages and the issues they touch will be *too* challenging. Naturally, we all resist change—I do—but beyond our natural resistance, there will be some for whom change in the art is especially abhorrent. These individuals are too deeply invested and entrenched in their particular systems and methods to even recognize the need for change, much less accept it. The ostrich may bury his head in the sand, but simply not seeing the truth never changes it. Recognized or not, accepted or no, the weeding *will* come.

◆ ◆ ◆

Before proceeding to the next chapters, it is necessary to establish a common vocabulary. Without one, you will quickly tire of the phrases, *martial art, fighting art,* and *self-defense-motivated martial artist.* Long phrases become irksome with repetition, so throughout the remainder of this book, where the term *martial artist* appears, it will mean a student of the art whose *primary* motivation for study and training is mastery of and excellence in self-defense. The terms *martial art* and *fighting art* will—except in the chapter that differentiates them—mean "an art whose primary or original focus is self-defense." This definition distinguishes the *art* from its evolutionary offspring, martial *ways* and martial *sports.* That said, let's begin.

ONE

Why Study Martial Arts?

For some time there has been a trend in the United States toward physical fitness. However, not everyone is completely satisfied with some of the more popular fitness programs. There are, for example, those who feel that jogging is beneficial, but that it is also boring. Weight training, in the traditional "iron works" sweatshop or the modern health club, offers health and strength benefits, but for some, this, too, leaves something to be desired. Then there are those who find aerobics an enjoyable way to improve fitness, but even they would prefer an exercise program with more purpose. In an effort to find something that meets their fitness goals in a unique, enjoyable, and potentially practical way, many turn to martial arts.

Asian martial arts are as diverse as they are popular. In the United States you can study fighting and martial arts from China, Korea, Japan, Okinawa, the Philippines, Indonesia, Thailand, Malaysia, Vietnam, and India.

The Chinese arts offer more variety (comprise more individual styles) than most of us can even imagine. They range broadly from the direct, often linear, rapid-fire, in-your-face wing chun, to the gymnastic and acrobatic modern wu shu, to the graceful, almost hypnotic t'ai chi ch'uan. And literally hundreds of distinct systems and styles fill the space between these three.

1

Then there are Korean arts which focus primarily on high kicking (those less flexible need not apply). The requirement for flexibility is one reason so many young people take up tae kwon do, Korea's national martial (and now an Olympic) sport. (The vast number of schools doesn't hurt the art's popularity either.)

Japanese karate came from Okinawa. Because of this, Japanese and Okinawan martial arts are often lumped together. But karate is not the only art to come from the Land of the Rising Sun. Japanese and Okinawan arts also include extensive classical weapons training as well as a suite of grappling styles (primarily judo, jujutsu, and aikido). Their weapons systems include bladed, impact, and throwing or projectile weapons like the classical Japanese sword, the grain flail or nunchaku, and the bow and arrow.

Indomitable in spirit, the Philippine islands have repeatedly endured foreign rule. Fighting arts and systems there developed with a strong focus on survival, so there is considerable emphasis on weapons training. Often the training in other Asian martial arts moves from empty-hand to weapons, but in the Philippines, just the opposite is true. There, the student begins with sticks and knives and moves to unarmed training. Among Filipinos there are nearly as many systems and styles as there are villages and masters. Still, they all fall within three major groupings: kali from the southern end of that island nation, arnis from the northern end, and escrima, practiced throughout the middle of the island chain. Here, too, the number of systems or distinct styles within these three major genres of Filipino arts number in the hundreds.

I haven't even scratched the surface here, and I've only touched on some of the better known Asian arts. Among the plethora of other martial arts available to us today: are the increasingly popular Brazilian jiujitsu; Brazilian capoeria; Malaysian bando; Korean tang soo do, hapkido and hwarang do; Japanese iaido; Indian kalaripayit; Okinawan kempo and Chinese kenpo; Japanese kendo; Chinese kuntao; Indonesian pentjak silat; French savate; and muay thai from Thailand. Of all these and more that are available (and again, this is the briefest of lists) stand-up striking arts such as karate remain the most popular in the United States. I use the term "karate" here in the most generic sense to mean, as it is defined by Webster's New Collegiate Dictionary, any *"Oriental art of self-defense in which an attacker is disabled by crippling kicks and punches."* Kung fu, tae kwon do, and a host of other arts are included under this broad definition.

Martial arts may be studied and practiced solely for fitness; however, what makes them an attractive alternative to other fitness programs is what they offer in their four main areas of expression: sport, philosophy, art, and self-defense. Historically, each expression developed in response to specific needs, and by looking at each one we can get a better feel for the broad attraction that the martial arts hold.

Martial Sports

For the practitioner and spectator alike, martial sports (particularly sport karate, tae kwon do, and wushu) are probably the most exciting facet of the martial arts. They are certainly the most visible. But to see where the "sport" fits into the art as a whole, we need to examine not only what martial sports are, but also, what they are not.

Any martial sport is, first and foremost, *a game played by martial artists.* Certainly, it is a game with martial roots and emphasis, and there is little doubt that what is being demonstrated can be effective, but it is still only a game. There are rules that control the techniques, targets, and degrees of contact allowed the participants. These artificial limits are used to insure the safety of the players, but because of these limitations, martial sports can, at best, represent or show only a fraction of the strategies, tactics and techniques that are taught and practiced in the art as a whole. In this respect, martial sports are like war games. Just as war games cannot fully represent the reality and depth of war, martial sports cannot represent the reality and depth of their respective arts.

The point here is that the highly visible sporting aspect of any martial art—sport karate, Olympic tae kwon do, full-contact kick-boxing, and so on—represents only the smallest part of that art. Much like the tip of

COURTESY BOB DAVIS, OMEGA KARATE

FIGURE 1–1   Traditional sport-karate.

an iceberg, the sporting element is the most visible, but it is not truly representative of the art as a whole. Martial sports are a part of the martial arts—not vice versa.

Still, with the right approach, the proper attitude, and the appropriate forum, participation in sporting and competitive events can contribute positively to the development of a well-rounded martial artist. Like other artisans, martial artists enjoy having their work appreciated. Martial games provide a platform for demonstrating the artist's skill. They offer the practitioner a chance for recognition among his peers. More important, sport competition provides an excellent opportunity to exchange ideas and learn from others of differing perspectives, styles, and opinions. This alone is reason enough for participating in the sporting aspect of the martial arts.

Martial Art Philosophies

A number of practitioners devote their lives to martial art study primarily for *self-cultivation.* Through their practice of the art, they seek to attain some glimpse of the "Wisdom of the East," as set forth in the various philosophies of Taoism, Buddhism, Zen, and the like. For example, many practitioners describe karate-do (the way of karate) as a journey that begins with the physical and ends with the spirit. The goal, for them, is development of the spirit. How? Through physical karate training. In this way, karate-do parallels hatha-yoga with its self-purification through physical application.

The incorporation of the contemplative, meditative, or philosophical elements into the art may have evolved as teachers began to see a need for morality among its highly skilled practitioners. As practitioners became increasingly capable of inflicting pain and substantial bodily injury—some form of control, some personal means of tempering physical conduct and actions—became necessary. The Japanese attempted this by developing the military-based moral code of *bushido* that eventually became the basis of ethical training for all of Japanese society.

For some, their art provides a sort of meditation in motion. This, they hope, will lead them to discover the wisdom needed to understand both themselves and the often unintelligible world in which they live. What they seek from the art is a philosophy of life, a code to live by, a discipline in an otherwise undisciplined world.

While the American melting pot welcomes new thoughts and ideas, it does not welcome them all. For example, for many Americans the idea of using martial art training as a means of discovering or formulating a philosophy to live by fails for at least two reasons. First, ours is a heterogeneous, highly diverse, and pluralistic society. We have, for example, numerous alternative avenues for those wishing to study Eastern culture, thought, and philosophy (and without having to break a sweat doing it, either). Second, and more important to some, Asian martial art philosophy is deeply entwined in Eastern mysticism and religion. As such, its spiritual

FIGURE 1–2

FIGURE 1–3 Iaido—meditation in motion.

5

and religious elements are often anathema to those holding other religious beliefs (this aspect of the art is addressed in detail in Chapter 11).

Aware of this potential cultural conflict, many American martial artists dismiss the religious overtones of their arts and concentrate on those aspects that will enhance mental concentration, improve sensitivity to differing degrees of threat, and increase awareness of the interaction between attitude and performance.

Martial Arts As Art

Interest in martial arts is also found among those who pursue martial art study as *art*. These individuals are interested in learning martial arts not for self-defense or sport, but as *art forms*. The student who studies a martial art as an art form is typically one who is also interested in the classical traditions, religions, philosophies, and meditational aspects of the art— areas that are generally of less interest to those studying the arts for practical self-defense. (Please note that I say "less" interest—not "*no*" interest.)

For myself, studying martial arts as art forms sounds a little like practicing basketball just for the sake of "the game." Doesn't a person practice basketball to "play the game?" True, we cannot go about beating people (playing our game), but we can participate in a variety of exercises that bring us closer to that reality. One who wishes to take up martial arts as an art would very likely enjoy the study of martial ways like classical aikido, iaido (a Japanese sword art) or kyudo (the way of the bow and arrow), or some other less practical martial art, such as Yang-style t'ai chi ch'uan (as commonly practiced for health—physical and mental). By "less

FIGURE 1–4   T'ai chi ch'uan player.

practical," I mean that to most Americans, the study of weapons like the sword or the Japanese bow and arrow are not very practical for self-defense because, for example, they cannot be stored, carried, or otherwise kept readily available for use if needed.

A martial art is an "art." It is not, however, an art form. It is a skill acquired by experience, study, and observation. Also, it is something that you can enjoy and participate in almost your entire life. But again, it is, first and foremost, an art of self-defense. Why else is it called "martial"?

Martial Arts for Self-Defense

Despite the attraction the other areas of the art have, self-defense remains the primary motivator for most who begin martial art study. I say this because even those who pursue martial arts for the reasons already discussed often say that they also took up the arts for their self-defense benefits.

Self-defense is not simply a pragmatic motivation for studying the arts, for beauty and art are inextricably intertwined in this, the original purpose of martial art development. Self-defense study is simultaneously stimulating and relaxing. It challenges us, demands more, and it rewards our efforts. In more than one way it is like health insurance. Practitioners are rewarded because not only do they benefit from the strenuous physical exercise, they also benefit from the skills and abilities they develop—skills that prepare them, should the need arise, to defend their lives and the lives of their loved ones. This kind of health insurance simply isn't available anywhere else.

The difference between those who "*also* took up martial arts for their self-defense benefits" and the student studying *primarily* for self-defense, is motivation. For all the other avenues self-defense-motivated martial artists may eventually take in their walks down the martial path, for all of the other interesting and exciting things they may eventually explore as they stay the course, one thing remains constant: the desire for confidence in their abilities to protect their families and themselves. This, coupled with the desire for excellence in this area, remains the *martial artist's* primary motivation for study and participation in the art.

Why Martial Arts?

Martial arts are so broad that they can be studied and practiced for fitness, sport, artistic endeavor, self-defense, or all of the above. This breadth of expression is part of the attraction they hold. But let me tell you in one word why most people take up martial arts: *choice.* We all lead busy lives, and making the most of our time is important. Most of us recognize the need for exercise but find most fitness programs just boring hard work. Martial art study and training is hard work, but while it is also good exercise, it is anything but boring. But martial art study offers something else that few exercise programs can match: *confidence.* Other exercise programs may strengthen your body, giving you more confidence in general, but martial art training breeds a level of confidence that springs only from the knowledge that you are not easily threatened or intimidated. In the street or in the board room, you now have choices. Untrained, you have no choice but submission. Trained, you choose whether to yield or stand your ground. This kind of choice is available only to those who first choose to study martial arts.

◆ ◆ ◆

A warrior may choose pacifism. Others are condemned to it.

TWO

The Evolutionary Cycle of Combat Arts

The system is not a fancy martial art, but a street-oriented brand of fighting. Hair pulling, neck grabbing, kicks to the back of the knee joint—they're all fair game in the system. ... No rules. No belts. No nonsense. The system is a fighting art without all the needless baggage.

—Mike Sturman, 1995
Black Belt magazine

In cyclical fashion, self-defense skills and systems of combat move through phases of evolution and devolution. During periods of violence and brutality, they evolve rapidly upward, gaining in sophistication and effectiveness. During times of relative peace and prosperity, they stagnate and slowly devolve downward. This chapter discusses where we are today in the evolutionary cycle and its impact on modern martial art training and development.

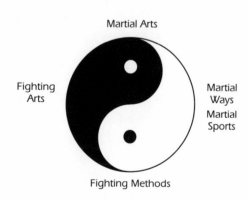

Martial Arts

Fighting Arts

Martial Ways
Martial Sports

Fighting Methods

Evolution

Any student of history knows that weapons of war and the skills to wield them only improve (if you can call it that), increasing in their destructive capability during periods of conflict and war. (Only in the most militaristic societies do they continue to evolve during peacetime.) This growth in military weapons and tactics has a parallel in the development and evolution of combat skills for individual and personal protection.

Fighting Methods to Fighting Arts

In an environment where fights are frequent, sudden, and often life-threatening, one does not have the luxury of practicing pain-compliance and control techniques. In this kind of environment, only those methods that are guaranteed to work, and work the first time, are studied and practiced. Collected and organized, these *fighting methods* become *fighting arts.*

Fighting arts are characterized by three words: *focus, reaction,* and *counterattack.* As a matter of survival in their harsh environments, practitioners of fighting arts must react to threats quickly and decisively—their *focus* is always on survival. Like the crocodile, the fighting art practitioner, when threatened or surprised, *reacts.* Assault is met not with defense but with *counterattack—* and one that ceases only when the opponent is vanquished. Fighting arts are violent, brutal, unforgiving, unrepentant, and extremely effective.

Fighting Arts to Martial Arts

As societies move from periods of conflict to periods of relative peace, *fighting art* development slows, and the system of combat gradually evolves into a *martial art.* Martial arts differ from fighting arts primarily in their sophistication and social interaction. Free from the pressure that demands an unwavering focus on survival, the martial artist devotes part of his valuable training time to actually understanding his art: analyzing its techniques, discovering why they work, and investigating their underlying principles.

Knowledge of an art's underlying principles is very important, for it yields the fruit of versatility. Versatility is the ability to apply a given

FIGURE 2–1   *Shearing* horizontal elbow strike to the head.

FIGURE 2–2   *Shearing* horizontal elbow strike to the upper arm.

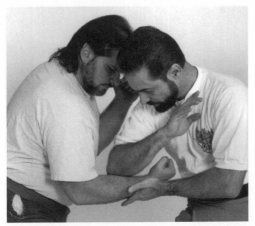

FIGURE 2–3   *Shearing* horizontal elbow strike to the forearm.

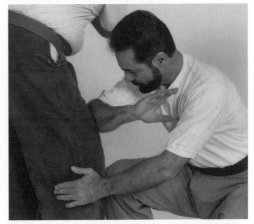

FIGURE 2–4   *Shearing* horizontal elbow strike to the leg.

movement (part of a technique) in more than one way. For example, one may practice a horizontal elbow strike to the head in such a way that uses a shearing action—one that applies two opposite, but parallel forces—(figure 2–1) and be completely unaware of the *shearing* principle.[1] However, once the underlying principle is understood, the movement is applicable to any number of targets (figures 2–2 through 2–4) and can be executed from more than one angle or plane.

Beyond the benefit of deeper knowledge and the versatility that goes with this, martial art practitioners also benefit from the development or rediscovery of completely different combative techniques—alternatives for dealing with confrontation and physical threat. To see what I mean, let's compare two techniques: one from a fighting art, the other, a martial art alternative.

In an environment where even peace overtures often precede ambush, the following technique makes perfect sense. Extending his hand in a gesture of peace, the antagonist declares a willingness to defuse a tense situation. Accepting his hand (figure 2–5), the defender remains cautious. Feeling a slight pull from his opponent and believing the gesture is only a ploy, the defender reacts quickly and decisively. Slapping his clasped hand to his right (figure 2–6), the defender lifts his opponent's arm, quickly steps under it (figure 2–7), and with a sharp pull down over his left shoulder, breaks his assailant's arm at the elbow (figure 2–8). Not only does this destroy his opponent's ability to continue his attack, but it also places the

FIGURE 2–5   In a mock gesture of peace, the antagonist shakes hands, but his intention is to thrust his knife (in the circle) into his intended victim.

FIGURE 2–6   The defender slaps the clasped hand to his right.

defender in a position where he can easily use his badly injured foe as a shield between himself and his assailant's still capable partner.

I call this approach to personal defense the *shotgun* method. This is because, at the slightest provocation, the defender (figuratively) blasts the attacker—as if with a shotgun. He makes no attempt to deter the opponent, gives no second chance; his goal is simply all-out destruction of the assailant's ability to fight.

If this technique appears particularly brutal, remember that it is used in a highly charged, hostile environment where violence is a way of life (and death). In this situation, you do what you must to survive. However, in an environment where the threat is normally not as great, the trained martial artist, with his broader arsenal of techniques, may find that the following technique works just as well—and without permanent damage to the antagonist.

As before, the antagonist extends his hand in a mock gesture of reconciliation (figure 2–9). Sensing a trap, the martial artist chooses a measured response (a choice the practitioner of the fighting art lacks). Slapping his clasped hand to the right, the defender pulls his antagonist's hand down and to the defender's hip (figure 2–10). Before his hapless opponent can

FIGURE 2–7   Lifting the assailant's arm high, the defender prepares to step under the extended arm.

FIGURE 2–8   Stepping under the assailant's outstretched arm, the defender breaks the arm over his shoulder.

13

FIGURE 2–9   In a mock gesture of peace, the antagonist shakes hands intending to pull his victim to his partner.

FIGURE 2–10   The defender slaps his clasped hand to his right, pulling it to his hip.

FIGURE 2–11   Feeding his hand back to him, the defender shoves his antagonist into his opponent's partner.

respond, the defender reverses the pull, lifting his opponent's hand, and applies a painful wrist lock [figure 2–11]. This maneuver gives the antagonist something to think about without (necessarily) inflicting permanent damage, while keeping the defender in the most defensible position (actually using the antagonist as a shield against his partner).

The martial artist really practices techniques from both camps: all-out counterattacks (figures 2–5 through 2–8] and pain compliance and control (figures 2–9 through 2–11]. The value of the fighting art technique is not lost on the martial artist. Although he initially responds with the pain-compliance technique, should it become necessary (as when a weapon is produced), the martial artist can quickly shift from his control tactic (figure 2–11) to one that completely destroys his assailant's arm (figures 2–12 and 2–13). The difference is that the martial artist has this option; the practitioner of the fighting art does not.

Options allow the martial artist to *respond* rather than *react*. Doubtless, under the tension of serious threat, with adrenaline flooding through

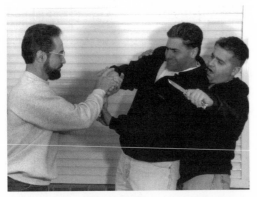

FIGURE 2–12 The defender continues to press his opponent into the armed partner as he simultaneous prepares to step under his arm.

FIGURE 2–13 Careful to keep his assailant between himself and the knife-wielding partner, the defender quickly neutralizes his nearest opponent.

his veins, the martial artist will, like the fighter, react. However, unlike the fighter, the martial artist's response is not limited to a narrow range of techniques designed only to kill or maim. The martial artist can, at any time, alter the direction of his defense anywhere along the way. Figuratively speaking, he may use the fighting artist's shotgun, but he can also choose a stick, a staff, a knife, or any other weapon in his broader arsenal. The fighting art practitioner, on the other hand, cannot. His shotgun is his only weapon, and it does not easily wound; it can only fire or hold fire.

Looked at another way, a martial art is a mature fighting art. It is polished and refined; sophisticated. Another military analogy is useful here. *Fighting arts*, with their methods of defense, are like saturation bombing—a brute-force method that strikes terror in the heart of the enemy. However, it does this only with maximum effort and resources. *Martial arts* are more like surgical strikes. They also get the job done, but like laser- and radar-guided precision bombing, they consume

FIGURE 2–14   B-52 Stratofortress.

15

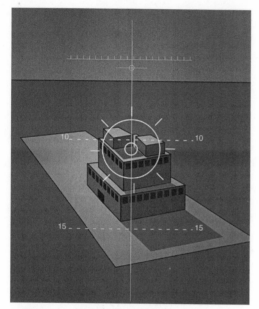

FIGURE 2–15   Laser- and radar-guided precision bombing.

fewer resources with significantly less collateral damage. Both methods are effective, and both are still used widely in modern warfare; however, one requires a significantly greater level of sophistication than the other. That one represents the *martial art.*

Social Interaction

Not to be lost in all of this is the fact that a martial art also differs from the fighting art in its social interaction. Socially, martial artists are made aware of the consequences of their responses to conflict. This awareness manifests itself in (among other things) the installation and teaching of codes of conduct—simple methods of controlling the behavior of the practitioner. Fighting arts, on the other hand, almost never have such codes (collateral damage is not their concern).

Remember, a fighting art practitioner's only goal is survival; social responsibility is not his concern. A martial artist's primary purpose is also survival, but unlike the fighting art practitioner, this crocodile looks before biting.

There are other differences between fighting and martial arts, but from the self-defense perspective, these are the major ones. A martial art, with its emphasis on understanding combat principles and its recognition of social responsibility, represents the peak of the evolutionary cycle. It is a proven and effective fighting art that has matured.

Devolution

From this top of the evolutionary cycle, martial art development begins to stagnate. Its original focus shifts from that of providing its practitioners with effective self-defense skills, to one that is more socially acceptable. As part of the natural cycle, the devolution now begins, and the *art* moves from martial *art* to either a martial *way* or martial *sport*. In the United States, we have entered this regression phase of the evolutionary cycle. Let's look for a moment at the latter half of this century and see just how we came to where we are today.

Much has changed since the days when Asian masters of fighting and martial arts routinely tested and practiced their combat-proven techniques. After World War II, global social developments altered the evolution of classical martial arts and, with it, martial art training. A new order of global peace and personal security was declared. To be sure, there was still violence, and too soon the nations of the world found themselves caught up in a cold war. But affluent Western powers still convinced their citizens that there was little need for *personal* self-defense.

FIGURE 2–16

This *Pax Romana* of modern time, coupled with the ban on Japanese martial arts during the American occupation of that country, meant that the days of empirical study of martial arts, there and elsewhere, were numbered. Challenges and fights-to-the-death to see whose art was the best went the way of the Old West gunfighter. All of this left contemporary martial artists with little more than *legend* and *lore* as the bases of their art's self-defense effectiveness and authenticity. Only those nations where one's life still depended on his martial prowess witnessed any continued martial art development.

In the West, martial *sports* have surpassed martial arts in both recognition and popularity. In the United States, for example, emphasis on the sporting element means that techniques and training methods are developed that teach the student how to score points. Martial effectiveness is sacrificed for sporting performance and trophies.

In the East, much of the *art* has been replaced by the martial *way*. For example, in Japan the degradation from martial *art* to martial *way* began with the restoration of the Meiji Emperor in 1867. Now, more than a century later, we find that warrior arts are no longer taught for development of martial skill. Martial arts like ken-jutsu, iai-jutsu, and kyu-jutsu became the martial ways of kendo, iaido, and kyudo—martial ways whose purpose for practice is self-development and perfection of character.[2]

In China, modern wushu, with its extended stances and gymnastic acrobatics, replaced many of that nation's previously effective classical fighting arts. Wushu players, like circus performers, are entertaining to watch and amazing in their physical ability, but the *efficacy* of their art as a self-defense system of combat has greatly diminished. This is because the understanding and interpretation of the original function and meaning of the classical movements have eroded with the passing of each master. For many Chinese systems today, masters of the classical period are the last practitioners of their arts who were intimately familiar with their arts' effectiveness, for they tested and witnessed their application, firsthand.

What this means to American practitioners is that while fighting continues on its ever-changing course (neighborhood thugs continually update their skills, and tournament players sharpen their skills for excellence within the narrow confines of the arena), the self-defense student is left to study and practice the techniques and tactics of the past.

FIGURE 2–17   Modern *wushu* has less in common with practical self-defense, than it does with dance or gymnastics.

Canonizing these observations into a "law of the art," we are forced to admit the following: *As the distance between the past and the present increases, the effectiveness of any classical fighting art decreases.* The result of all of this is that, with each new generation, *actual knowledge* of tested and proven combat and self-defense effectiveness moves ever-deeper into the realm of myth.

Breaking the Cycle

The deterioration of martial art effectiveness would likely have continued unabated for some time, were it not for the efforts of modern martial art pioneers. These dedicated individuals broke the yoke of tradition to focus and shape martial arts in America. Like the masters of the past, these men studied their arts empirically. They experimented, observed, and experienced the theories they discovered. (And yes, a large amount of their experimentation, observation, and experience came from real head-thumping fights.)

Notice I said that these men "discovered," and not that they *developed* or *created.* This is because practically everything that can be done to the human body with regard to personal self-defense has already been tested or experienced. For example, there are only so many ways a fist or hand can come at you: hook, cross, straight, over the top, and uppercut. In response, there is only a finite number of ways to deflect, defend against, or otherwise manipulate the attacking arm. Because these things remain constant, there is really very little *new,* revolutionary *development.* There is, however, *rediscovery.*

Rediscovery

Rediscovery results from analyzing classical techniques and patterns of movement in context. Contrary to some of what Lee advocated, the intelligent martial artist actually discards very little. He may take a classical technique, movement, or form and set it aside to be revisited later, but he will only rarely discard it outright. A jump sidekick, for example, had a specific purpose when it was first developed, and we need to understand it in the context of that period of history—learning why it was necessary—to discover its usefulness and applicability today. Banishing any work as useless only demonstrates the martial artist's lack of understanding. We may not have experienced or understood the conditions that spawned a classical technique and proved its effectiveness, and we cannot go about testing our theories by pounding everyone we don't like into the dirt, but we do have some advantages that past masters did not.

Modern Advantages

Growing up in Indonesia during World War II, my Dutch-Indonesian instructor did not enjoy the luxury of training with safety equipment. If a

student in his day made a mistake when practicing his technique, it often cost him dearly; he could be scarred for life or, worse, crippled. While this harsh training environment made fighting art practitioners tougher, it also made for fewer of them.

To help us in our quest to understand and apply classical techniques, modern practitioners make full use of technological advances not available to previous generations. We use specialized training equipment, safety gear, and video technology. Modern training equipment helps us improve our quickness and timing, stretch our muscles and joints with greater frequency and less chance of injury, and do all this for many more years than was previously possible.

Advances in safety equipment allow us to try techniques and movements hundreds and thousands of times without the risk of serious injury. Practitioners today can repeatedly practice techniques that, just a decade ago, would have prematurely ended their training if they made even the smallest mistake. Technology, then, gives modern practitioners a considerable advantage.

FIGURE 2–18   Training "safety" equipment.

EQUIPMENT COURTESY TIGRON MARTIAL ART SUPPLY, DENVER, COLORADO

Equally significant is the fact that, in the United States, we may train in many different fighting and martial arts. The "shrinking of our world" means we have access to many, many more arts than our predecessors did. Greater exposure to different approaches to combat gives greater flexibility in confrontational situations. You can choose, for example, from an aikido redirection technique, a pain-compliance from jujutsu, or a leg kick from Thai-boxing. Open access to so many arts is something only dreamed of by past masters.

Modern video equipment is another benefit today's martial artist enjoys. Access to video cameras and tape players allows us to study techniques, forms, and patterns of movement over and over again. Training tapes sharing other arts were unthinkable just a generation ago. What do you think Okinawan karate masters would have given for this kind of resource?

FIGURE 2–19   Video equipment, a modern training aid.

All of this means that today's martial artist is in an excellent position to study, analyze, and comprehend classical martial art techniques and their underlying principles of movement. Parker and Lee, both well ahead of their time, made excellent use of video equipment. As American martial artists, then, it is in our best interests to bring the study of martial arts into the twenty-first century, using every tool available to us. This means utilizing technology and other advances in training equipment. More importantly, it means using our God-given minds. In other words, don't park your brains at the dojo door.

Recycling

You can see how self-defense skills and systems of personal combat develop and decline in cyclical fashion. They evolve rapidly upward, gaining in sophistication and effectiveness during periods of violence and brutality. In peacetime they stagnate and slowly devolve downward into either martial *ways* or martial *sports*. Asian martial arts in America are in the devolution phase of the evolutionary cycle. *Actual knowledge* of the classical Eastern combat skills that American students are learning is beyond our reach. This is because most of the men who were intimately familiar with them have passed away. Our fascination with martial sports only compounds the problem. Many practitioners today learn how to score points instead of how to survive real confrontations. Martial ways, with their emphasis on character perfection rather than self-protection, offer little help for the self-defense motivated martial artist. This is the current state of martial arts in America. However, we need not settle for the status quo.

Our culture and environment may be far removed from those that spawned the potent arts we are so fortunate to have available to us today, and we may not be able to test our fighting theories as past masters did (empirically—by busting heads), but development and discovery are still available to the dedicated student of the art. This is because we in the West enjoy unprecedented access to more Asian fighting and martial art systems than any who trained before us. And second, we have technological advantages that would boggle the minds of past martial art masters. Used properly, video recording equipment and modern training gear can do for students of Asian martial arts what similar advances have done for modern Olympic champions. No, the downward slide in martial art development in America need not continue; the status need not remain quo.

THREE

Preserving Ancient Arts

Yip Man[1] admitted himself that he changed *wing chun* from what he had learned and continued to modify the art up until the day he died.

—Dennis Dickens, 1993
Inside Kung-Fu magazine

O f all the obstacles the American martial artist encounters in his quest for effective self-defense, none loom larger than the giant called *preservation*. Preservation of an ancient skill is a noble objective, and it has its place in the martial arts; however, for the modern martial artist, such a goal is often counterproductive. Beginning with a look at preservation in general (listing, briefly, the types of things we preserve and why), this chapter moves quickly to an examination of one place where this otherwise admirable effort is at cross-purposes with the goals of today's self-defense-motivated martial art practitioner.

Preservation: A Universal Need

There is in man a universal need to preserve elements of his past. This includes both accomplishments that we're proud of and atrocities we're ashamed of.

FIGURE 3–1   Constitution of the United States.

Good and bad, all of them give meaning to life and chronicle the human experience.

We preserve, for example, important acts and significant *historical events*—events that, although they occur once in time, impact lives and alter the course of history. Historical declarations like the Magna Carta, and the American Constitution and Declaration of Independence fall into this category. *Places* that remind us of the past (both famous and infamous) also warrant preservation: the Parthenon, Machu Picchu, the Roman Coliseum, the Jamestown settlement, and, yes, even Dachau and Auschwitz. These events and places remind us of where we've been, cause us to reflect on where we are, and to consider where we're going. They also remind us of where we should never tread again. The *timeless works* of past masters like Da Vinci, Michelangelo, and Rodin enrich our lives with their artistic power. The classical compositions of Mozart, Beethoven, and Bach represent great peaks in musical history. These great works, along with those of literary giants like Shakespeare, Cervantes, and many others, all merit our efforts to save, protect, and preserve them.

But events, places, and great works of the arts and humanities are not the only things we preserve. Past *skills* are equally worthy of protection. Although some are no longer needed for the advancement and prosperity of society today, many are worthy of preservation because of their significant contributions to our history and development. Japanese sword smithery, Damascene and Toledo metallurgy, Roman engineering, and many others fall into this category.

Beyond commemorating our past, preserving ancient skills enriches and even safeguards our future. For example, powered vessels using satellite-based global positioning systems (GPS) have largely replaced sailing ships and the need for compass and sextant. However, modern advancements aside, it is still in our best interest to preserve these ancient mariner skills, for who can say with certainty that we will never need them again?

Because of their contributions to mankind's development and history, we preserve significant acts, events, great works of the arts and humanities, and skills of man's ingenuity. Likewise, because of their contributions to their arts' development and history, there are also things that martial art practitioners preserve. Here are a few.

Where Preservation Makes Sense

The preserved techniques of the Japanese sword, the bow and arrow, and the halberd, found in the martial ways of iaido, kyudo, and naginata-do, are examples of ancient arts where preservation makes sense. It makes sense because their skills are no longer taught as martial arts for self-defense. Practiced now as martial ways, with an emphasis on character building and the development of inner peace, what were previously combat arts now play very different roles in society.

FIGURE 3–2   Rodin's Thinker.

Preservation of arts like these make sense because their development as self-defense systems ceased long ago. Their devolution from martial arts to martial ways—hastened by the increased effectiveness of modern weapons—rendered these once potent classical Japanese weapons impractical for self-defense in twentieth-century urban environments.

Practitioners of these arts may dispute the contention that they are no longer effective for self-defense, arguing that the weapons in question are still lethal. In this, they are correct; the Japanese *katana* or sword is, indeed, a formidable weapon. However, there are compelling reasons why

FIGURE 3–3   Some ancient weapons are impractical today.

weapons like the sword, the staff, the halberd, and others are, nonetheless, impractical today as self-defense weapons and systems of personal defense—principally, the difficulty in transporting and accessing them.

Realistically, carrying around a six-foot staff or eight-foot-long halberd in one's car or on a crowded bus is simply impractical—not to mention quickly whipping the thing out when you need it. Carry a samurai sword with you down the street and you will very likely be stopped and questioned by police so frequently that you may never arrive at your destination.

Ancient Japanese arts aren't the only ones facing this reality. The idea of carrying even some of the smaller, more exotic weapons, like the Chinese deer-antler knife or butterfly sword, or Filipino *kris* under your coat or in your briefcase is none too practical either—especially if they're ready for use (sharpened). For arts and weapons like these, preservation makes sense because their value as self-defense weapons and systems of combat has long since been surpassed by their cultural and historical value. From the modern martial artist's perspective, preserving these arts is no problem. For us, the issue becomes a problem when people try to preserve arts that are still capable of providing practical self-defense.

When Preservation Destroys

Regardless of the motivation behind your desire for preservation, the fact remains that preserving any truly effective self-defense art inevitably destroys (rather than preserves) the very attributes and characteristics that make it a candidate for preservation in the first place. Study martial arts long enough and you realize that what made past masters great was not how they preserved their teachers' arts, but their willingness to *adapt* and *change* them. This is a large part of the reason they were masters and the principal reason the arts they practiced remain effective. These men of vision realized that hanging on to the old ways of fighting meant certain doom—for them and their way of life. Adapting to change was, and still is, the only way to survive—in business, in everyday life, as an individual, and especially as a martial artist.

This desire to preserve the teacher's art is not just a Japanese, Chinese, or Korean thing. Many fine practitioners from any number of Asian cultures fall prey to what is otherwise a noble goal. For example, I know instructors of both Indonesian and Filipino extract whose stated purpose in sharing their martial art knowledge is the advancement and preservation of their (or their teacher's) heritage and culture. I fully support the preservation of one's heritage and cultural traditions; however, I think it unreasonable to expect those of another culture to adopt the same goal for a culture that is not their own. If, for example, a Brazilian teaching jiu-jitsu seeks to preserve his Brazilian heritage and culture as part of his instruction, is it reasonable for him to ask his German-, Lithuanian-, and Mexican-American students to also preserve his cultural heritage? I think not. If, on the other hand, one's martial *art* is actually a martial *way*, where the purpose is self-improvement, perfection of character, or spiritual enlightenment, then preservation is, again, reasonable.

Preserving Adaptability—An Oxymoron

Let's begin by asking ourselves this question. Does the preservationist do his masters a service or a disservice by preserving their techniques—exactly as they were taught? I believe that if we are dealing with a martial *art* (one that still claims self-defense effectiveness), then we do them grave disservice.

FIGURE 3–4

Taking a self-defense or combat art and preserving it—freezing it in time—is like taxidermy. You take an animal that is vibrant, exciting, and full of life. It may be beautiful, powerful, cunning, or breathtakingly terrifying. Preserving it (remember, you have to kill it before you can preserve it), reduces the beast to a mere shell of what it once was. On the outside, it may look like its former self, but in reality it is less—much, much less—than what it was in life. There is a world of difference between a live 10-foot-tall, 1,200 pound grizzly bear and one displayed in a museum. In the diorama the grizzly stands: clean and well groomed; without scent, sweat, or smell—well preserved, *but lifeless.*

I remember finding a small beetle once. It appeared to have a body made of iridescent gold and silver. Each section of its body was delineated by a thin black line. It was incredibility beautiful. I gave the beetle to a friend who thought she would preserve its beauty by sealing it in plastic (we both thought the creature was dead). Placing the beetle in the liquid plastic, we discovered it was, indeed, alive! By that time, however, it was too late and the beetle died. Amazingly, as the creature expired, its beautiful shell diminished and all the gold and silver vanished. It looked now like an ordinary bug. You see, the real beauty (or terror) in any living thing is in its *life.* A martial art is exactly like that!

Consider boxing. Does anyone believe that Julio Caesar Chavez could have beaten Hector "Macho" Camacho using the preserved techniques of past boxing greats like John L. Sullivan or Jim Corbett? Of course not. Boxing is a self-defense art. Its weapons are limited to the hands, but it is a self-defense art nonetheless. I say this because boxers hit each other—all the time. If a boxer does not defend himself against his opponent in the ring (even in practice), he will have his head handed to him. Every sparring session then, is a self-defense lesson, and boxers know that you cannot fight today's fighters with yesterday's techniques.

You can still honor past masters *without* preserving the techniques of their art. Instead, we acknowledge their *contributions* and their *skills*. We honor Jim Corbett and John L. Sullivan, but we no longer box as they did. We build on their foundation and preserve the timeless *principles* of the masters' art, but we must not remove the very life from their art by preserving its *techniques*. An excellent example of what can happen when you do is found in modern *jeet kune do*.

FIGURE 3–5　John L. Sullivan, 1858–1918.

The Jeet Kune Do Example

Two camps have evolved from Bruce Lee's stable. Both preserve his name, but one continues to honor him by growing and evolving with his ideas, while the other attempts to do the same by preserving his original techniques. Preserving his techniques is contrary to what Lee advocated in life. Those who have preserved Lee's teachings, principles, and concepts continue to grow—and have added even greater proportion to Lee's already legendary stature.

FIGURE 3–6　Jeet kune do's creator, Bruce Lee.

Sabres And Samurai

In life, the only constant is change, and martial arts must change as well. The cavalry sabre evolved into the foil of the gentry because gentlemen rarely, if ever, faced armored opponents. When a gentleman used his weapon, it was *not* against someone wearing, for example, a breastplate. The foil was designed to penetrate cloth and flesh, not armor, and techniques for its use evolved accordingly. The development of the popular samurai sword followed a similar path.

FIGURE 3–7

Before the Tokugawa Shoguns, most Japanese swords were much heavier, for they were designed to smash through armor. With relative peace restored to Japan, the samurai wore less and less armor, thereby changing the requirements for the sword. Blades were made both lighter and sharper because they needed only slash through lightweight materials to inflict their disabling or killing blow. Schools of kenjutsu and iai-jutsu developed wholly new techniques because of this evolution. The use of two swords also became practical because you no longer needed both hands to hold the weapon in an attempt to drive it through the armor that formed the "turtle's shell."

Martial art training and study preserve the *tradition of change* by adapting to the ever-changing combat environment. In peacetime, "combat-proven techniques" (i.e., military and counterterrorism techniques) are reserved for those needing them. This does not exclude them from the civilian martial artist's arsenal; it just keeps them in context. The preservationist's goal is commendable, but it is ill-conceived when it comes to effective martial art systems and techniques.

We honor past martial art masters by continuing the tradition that is the strength of their arts—namely, the tradition of adaptation and change. Filipino and Indonesian martial arts remain effective today because of *that* tradition. Do that, and you pay the greatest honor to those masters and their arts. Preserve their arts in their original form and, rest assured, in just one generation you will have reduced them to little more than museum pieces. Were they to return from the dead, I believe the great masters would much rather see their arts still alive and growing than preserved *and lifeless.*

FOUR

Lethal Skill at a
Friday Night Party

Destroy your attacker using never-before-seen 'killing' techniques. Creator of *Official* U.S. Navy SEAL combat system releases brutal *Gun & Knife* sections of his Instructor Qualification Fighting Series.

SEAL team hand-to-hand combat and weapons training. The ultimate self-defense system.

—Advertisements, May, 1996
Black Belt magazine

The previous chapter dealt with the issue of preserving an ancient fighting or martial art for the purposes of honoring the art's founder and maintaining cultural roots. There remains, however, another oft-used and outwardly compelling argument for preserving a fighting art: combat effectiveness. Practitioners holding this belief may likewise seek to honor their arts' founders, but not for the reasons already discussed. Their reasoning is that since the techniques of their arts' founders were effective in what is undeniably the most extreme fighting environment, war, surely they must be the best techniques for self-defense. But are they really? This chapter examines this popular combat/preservation connection by posing the following:

1. Apart from their possible historical or cultural value (already addressed in the preceding chapter), is there merit in preserving "combat" arts and their techniques?
2. Is an instructor's success with his techniques (combat-proven or otherwise) sufficient reason for maintaining them exactly as received?
3. Are combat arts and techniques suitable for everyone?

Among martial artists, there is a clear distinction between "self-defense" training and training for "combat." Self-defense-oriented martial artists are not Rambo wannabes; they are craftsmen whose labors produce *practical* self-defense skills. Often, in describing self-defense capabilities of a system or technique, martial artists will use the term "combat effectiveness." Taken in context, this is understood to mean "street" or self-defense effectiveness. There is, however, a group for whom the term "combat" means exactly that—military or paramilitary skills employed by professional soldiers—and it is *this* use of the term that we examine in this chapter.[1]

Combat Effectiveness as the Standard

Combat effectiveness has long been the standard by which techniques and martial art systems are measured. I have a friend, for example, who believes that techniques that are or have been proven in combat should never be changed, precisely because their effectiveness has received the highest seal of approval; they passed the "ultimate" test. He uses his late instructor as an example.

My friend's teacher was a professional soldier—a member of one of our elite fighting forces. His credentials were built on the fact that, while on active duty in Vietnam, he had, in the performance of his unit's mission, many opportunities to use his hand-to-hand fighting skills in actual life-and-death combat. You can see why many view this kind of "trial by combat" as the ultimate test of any technique, and their arguments have a measure of logic to them. I mean, what more can be said of any fighting system than that its techniques are "proven in combat?"

The argument is not new. Many practitioners have used it as their reason for preserving *ancient* arts. My friend's reasoning sounds somehow different because it is so contemporary, so relevant. Remember, this instructor's proving ground was Vietnam. As such, his skills and fighting methods cross both classical and contemporary lines. They were used successfully in our time and by a Western martial artist who was a practitioner of an old but very effective Asian fighting art. The blend of East and West is amplified when we consider that this modern warrior was himself of Dutch-Indonesian extract. That said, the question remains: *is combat effectiveness alone sufficient reason for maintaining any technique exactly as received?*

Changing Combat Techniques

Fighting is dynamic; it changes with the environment, with the enemy, with the culture, and with the weapons available to the combatants. For example, before American aircraft and armor could be used effectively in the Persian Gulf War, they had to be repainted to blend in with the desert environment. Moreover, since our equipment was designed for use in greener, cooler climates—not in desert sand and not in that kind of heat—we had to make substantial changes to the hardware if we expected to function and succeed in that new combat environment. This type of change is *environmental.* Other changes are forced on us by our enemies.

During the American Revolution, British inflexibility cost them the war. Even the best-trained, best-equipped army in the world could not win a guerrilla war while steadfastly wearing their bright red coats and marching in tight formation. The unalterable fact is that when it comes to fighting, we either change and adapt to our enemies' tactics, or face certain defeat. This is true for regional conflicts, and it is equally true for personal self-defense. The following excerpt from *Inside Karate* magazine (Lowry, 1987) contains an excellent example of the kind of changes I am talking about:

> It's common to see methods of attacking an opponent from the rear; slipping up, grabbing him and slitting his throat with a horizontal knife slash. In our era this may be effective, but claims that

FIGURE 4-1

it and techniques like it are part of a feudal ryu are incorrect. Attempting such a strike against a samurai would have been disastrous since they wore a gorget (nodowa) attached to their helmet or had armor covering the chin to the throat area in order to protect from that very kind of attack. In authentic bujutsu ryu, knife attacks against the throat are invariably stabbing ones and include a corresponding wrench with the other hand, meant to lift the gorget and twist it away.

An example of how an *unarmed* technique common today would have been impractical yesterday, appeared in an article on ninjutsu in *Black Belt* magazine. According to the article, ninjutsu authority Stephen Hayes states that the roundhouse kick is not included in the traditional ninja arsenal of personal weapons. As Hayes explains it, this is because the targets we commonly strike with a roundhouse kick today "would have been armored in the old days, so there wouldn't have been any reason to put a foot there" (Breen, 1995, 146).

Each of the two preceding examples point out how some of the techniques we use today would be ineffective in yesterday's combat environment. Doubtless, there are also techniques from bygone days that will not work effectively today.

Curiously, my friend proudly acknowledges the fact that the skills and system of his highly decorated instructor are based on his changes, and his blending of both the art he learned from his father (Chinese kuntao) and the art he adopted later in life (tae kwon do). However, to my friend, the idea of changing the art further—to better fit his individual characteristics and the world in which he lives—is unthinkable.

FIGURE 4–2

What's Good For The Goose . . .

The fact that my friend's teacher was wise enough to effectively blend the arts he had received and organize them into a system that worked for him begs the question, "Is the fact that any individual is successful with his techniques sufficient reason for his student to be *forever bound* to practice it and teach it *the same way?*" Hopefully you already have several good reasons for answering "no," but if you're still unsure, consider this. When analyzing the fighting style of any individual, you must understand the interaction between the techniques he employs, his physical abilities, and his personal traits. That individual's unique personal attributes may make the technique effective for him, but not for you.

For example, my instructor—whose shins have smashed through much more than I care to imagine—does not hesitate to do a shin-to-shin sweep. But for someone who sits behind a desk all day, even if he trains several times a week, is such a technique desirable? Are techniques that are used by any master, teacher, or talented individual necessarily suitable for everyone right out of the box? Often the answer is no.

Techniques a big man uses are seldom as effective when attempted by a smaller individual. The principles employed by any fighter may not be as sound or effective when used by another. For example, many boxing fans admired Joe Frazier, but how many of them would want to fight as he did? Frazier's fighting style was to stand in there—taking the best his opponent could give, while, hopefully, giving back more. How many of us can take that kind of punishment? How many of us even want to?

In the same light, how much of what past Okinawan masters like Kanryo Higashionna and Chojun Miyagi did was based on, or effective because of, their unique individual abilities? How much was effective because of their natural strength, size, muscle speed or reflexes? You see, what works for a great martial artist will not necessarily work for everyone. What worked for past masters, of *any* era, is not guaranteed to work for us today. The principles involved may be sound and have broad application; but again, we must carefully evaluate every art in light of its purpose—combat, self-defense, sport, or exercise—*and* the originator's or teacher's abilities. We must also consider the cultural and social context in which they were developed and effectively used.

Asian fighting and martial arts are extremely potent, and many of the techniques they use were, at various times, "proven in combat." But many of them were also developed a long time ago, in a very different environment, and for a people as culturally distant from ourselves today as their countries are geographically.

Cultural Differences

Historically, practitioners of classical (preserved) martial arts have simply chosen to ignore cultural differences. Nevertheless, the differences between the fighting methods employed by Americans and those demonstrated in most classical arts is undeniable. Even to the casual observer, it becomes quickly obvious that Americans simply do not fight like Asians—classical or contemporary. This is easy to understand when you consider the fact that Americans, today, do not fight as we did just a few decades ago. Thirty years ago, anyone kicking to the groin was a "dirty" fighter. Today, the groin is one of the first things savvy fighters attack.

Comparing East with West, we find that Americans are typically "head hunters." That is, given the choice, we prefer hitting the general where he lives: in the head. Most classical Asian martial arts, on the other hand, emphasize attacks to the body (the obvious exception is those sports that emphasize kicking to the head). Moreover, Americans prefer punching with the right hand with the left foot forward. (Among practitioners of Asian martial arts, this is referred to as a right reverse punch [figure 4–3].) Classical Asian martial arts, on the other hand, display a strong preference for the right lunge punch (figure 4–4)—one which, for example, brings the rear right leg forward as the right fist or hand strikes. These examples reflect cultural differences that are rarely considered when we evaluate the effectiveness of classical "combat" techniques.

FIGURE 4–3   The American "head hunter."

FIGURE 4–4   Classical horizontal punch to the body favored by many classical Asian martial artists.

Objectives

Beyond the technical, individual, and cultural differences that exist between the combat techniques of the past and today's reality, there remains yet another reason why "combat" effectiveness (classical or contemporary) is a poor argument for preserving a fighting system or specific technique: namely, the objectives of the practitioner himself.

The objectives of a soldier and those of the civilian martial artist are vastly different. According to lifelong professional soldier Lewis "Major Mike" Williams, "a soldier's job is to kill and break things. And that," he adds, "will never change." Death of the enemy and destruction of his ability to wage war are the soldier's primary objectives.

When an infantryman charges enemy ground, any head popping up in front of him is *always* assumed to be hostile. Saddam Hussein's human-shield warfare aside, the soldier does not normally expect to face innocent civilians on the battlefield. For this reason, he is given considerable latitude in the use of lethal force. (This "license to kill" is the main reason our military does not play a greater role in our national "War on Drugs.")

In war, combat techniques are effective *only* if they can kill, and kill quickly. This is the *sole standard* by which they are judged. In a combat environment, any technique that does not immediately neutralize an enemy is ineffective. (Combat is not the place to demonstrate the finer points of one's art.) However, this is not the case for the civilian martial artist. His situation is nearer that of civil authorities.

Unlike the soldier, the policeman works in a "friendly," peacetime environment, populated mostly with noncombative civilians (a debatable fact in some metropolitan areas, I am sure). In the performance of his job, the police officer must differentiate between the good guys and the bad guys. Because of this, he cannot respond to everyone he meets as if each is a hostile or lethal threat. The peace officer's primary objective is not wholesale death and destruction; it is service, protection, and maintenance of civil order. The same is true for the civilian martial artist.

FIGURE 4–5

When the civilian martial artist uses his skills in self-defense, his primary goal is to escape injury while protecting himself and others. His action may or may not require lethal force, but unlike the professional soldier, he views killing as his last option—not his first. Like the police officer, the civilian martial artist's response is dictated by circumstances such as the severity of the attack, the number of assailants, the use or absence of weapons, and the need to protect himself and others. Unlike the peace officer, the citizen is without the authority to dispense justice, so while his response is dictated by similar circumstances, his authority to punish is not.

Rough Riders Forever?

Were I still in the marines, I would take little comfort in knowing that I was learning "combat proven" techniques if they were the same ones our troops used during the Spanish-American War. Eastern or Western, the changes in warfare and personal combat that have occurred in the hundred years since Teddy Roosevelt charged San Juan Hill, are far too dramatic to warrant our entrusting our very survival to preserved combat techniques (of any culture). "Preserving combat techniques" is as oxymoronic as such oft-repeated phrases as *centered around, pretty ugly,* and *criminal justice.* All of them sound OK initially, but each is completely and totally illogical when examined more closely.

There is much that we can learn from the numerous fighting systems that were developed and taught by men who were obviously masters of their respective arts (past and present). We should study and record their techniques carefully, for these individuals serve as excellent sources of real experience. But their success with their fighting methods in no way guarantees their technique's effectiveness for everyone else—especially as the distance between their time and ours increases.

One final note with regard to making "combat" effectiveness the standard by which systems and techniques are measured. Just as grenade launchers and mortars are not the primary weapons of our civil authorities, neither are real "combat" techniques the *primary* tools of the civilian martial artist. This does not mean that martial art instructors should not teach such techniques. Techniques designed to kill an attacker are a legitimate part of the civilian martial artist's arsenal; they simply should not be the only part—or even a major part. In a military context, lethal skill is not a luxury; it is an absolute necessity. However, for the ill-advised or poorly trained civilian martial artist, *lethal skill at a Friday night party is the stuff of which nightmares are made.*

The argument that a fighting system should be preserved simply because its techniques have been proven in combat is flawed for two reasons. First, because—as was pointed out in Chapter 3—preserving any martial art or fighting system is the surest way to reduce its effectiveness as a combat art. Second, and more important, techniques designed solely to kill or neutralize an enemy quickly are far more dangerous in a civilian environment than they are useful. Clearly, they are useful—even necessary—but they are more dangerous because, in the overwhelming number of situations the civilian martial artist finds himself in, *death* as his response to threat is literally *overkill.* With the exception of the military professional, today's martial artist is not practicing his art as a soldier on the battlefield, but as a *civilian.*

FIVE

The Value of Tradition

In the evolutionary cycle of combat arts, as fighting methods evolve upward into martial arts, several changes take place. Beyond the purely technical transformations, there is the introduction of principles for governing the conduct of the practitioner. How these teachings manifest themselves in the art today—and their value to the American martial artist—is the focus of this chapter.

From the perspective of personal defense, the development of Western martial arts lagged far behind that of their Eastern counterparts. The cause of this unequal evolution is complex and beyond the scope of this chapter; however, the result is that Eastern martial arts reached a much higher developmental plane than any in the West. Not only were Eastern martial arts far ahead of the West on the physical scale, but they exceeded them in the intellectual, moral, and spiritual realm as well. This intellectual and moral development in Asian martial arts is visible today primarily through strong martial art traditions.

Of all the Asian martial art traditions, the most valuable relate to character development. These traditions teach concepts and attitudes such as justice, mercy, courage, kindness, courtesy, honesty, duty, loyalty, honor, obligation, responsibility, self-control, perseverance, respect for others, respect for parents, and respect for teachers. Some feel that the martial arts would be better off without these "peripheral" traditions ("let's just get down to crashin'-and-bashin' "), and considering how other martial traditions have been abused in the West, you can see their point.

For example, the requirement by many instructors to be addressed as "master"—or any other honorific title—is offensive to many American students. It is not so much the addressing of someone as "master" that is particularly offensive, as it is the *requirement* to do so. In our culture, respect, honor, and loyalty are things that are earned, not demanded. Moreover, in any country—certainly in an affluent one—a martial art teacher will very likely have students whose skills in their fields of expertise and professions far exceed his own skill in the art. How many instructors have attorneys, physicians, engineers and other professionals as students? Who, then, addresses whom as master?

In the West, true masters are seldom addressed as "master." Such individuals may be described as a masters of eminent skill, but with few exceptions, addressing one as "master" is considered pretentious and generally bad form. Setting aside such examples of tradition-abuse, there remain some very compelling reasons for maintaining the character-building traditions inherent in the martial arts.

Weeds

Perhaps the best reason for keeping these moral maxims is the fact that *where there are no positive traditions, negative ones appear.* This is always the case. Look at the natural world. On fertile ground, in the absence of welcome vegetation, weeds all too quickly appear. (Weeds, rather than grass, are always the first to fill the bare spots in a lawn.) The social parallel of this is found in Western boxing and wrestling. Lacking positive, character-building traditions of their own, Western martial arts have adopted a host of negative ones—especially in the professional ranks.

In professional wrestling, verbal abuse and public character assassination are the norm. These personal attacks are many times more vicious than the physical abuse the combatants inflict on each other in the ring. It matters not that none of this is taken seriously; it has, nevertheless, become a full-fledged Western martial art tradition.

Professional boxing is little better. The success of a fight—at least in financial terms—is measured as much by the verbal jabs and blows each fighter lands in the days and weeks preceding the fight as it is by the contest itself. Movie-goers will recall that the entire *Rocky* series is staged with exactly this type of hype and personal conduct as the backdrop—hardly professional.

FIGURE 5–1

Training Versus Teaching— The Instructor's Duty

Former heavyweight boxing champion Mike Tyson is a superbly trained fighter, and like many fight fans, I enjoy watching this mauling machine destroy his opponents in the ring. However, his conduct outside the ring (and not just in the criminal case that sent him to prison) suggests that his training did little to prepare him for life. This is the biggest shortcoming of modern Western martial art training. In the next century, sociologists studying this issue may point to some deep cultural and social differences as the cause for this state of affairs in Western martial arts, but I think the answer is much simpler than some exhausting doctoral thesis might conclude. I believe that in Western martial arts we have too many coaches, too many trainers, and too many managers—but far too few "teachers."

Trainers, as good as they are, only impart and sharpen skills; they *train*. Teachers, on the other hand, bestow much, much more than just physical skill. Let me show you what I mean.

When an individual attends college or university, often there is the assumption that he will receive training. I entered college after eighteen years in the work force. I remember thinking, "OK, I'll go to college and get a degree that says I can do what I am already doing." However, if the institution lives up to its mission (as mine did), then the student receives far more than just *training*; he receives an *education*. This is the major difference between a trade school and a college or university. In trade school, you receive training; in college, you receive an education. This highlights exactly the difference between trainers and teachers. Trainers and coaches *train*. Teachers also train, but, equally important, they *educate*.

Education is *very* different from training. The formal definitions of "education" and "training," as stated by Webster's make this clear. Training means, *to make proficient by instruction and practice, as in some art, profession, or work.* Education, on the other hand, is much more comprehensive. It is *the act or process of imparting or acquiring general knowledge, developing powers of reasoning and judgment, and generally preparing oneself or others intellectually for mature life.*

For all of the training the martial artist may acquire, his goal and that of his instructor should be education. Education is wrought at the hands of a capable and thorough teacher; not simply a trainer or coach. The teacher educates, preparing the student for life; the trainer does not. For example, you may be trained in the use of weapons and still not be trusted with them. Training develops primarily technical proficiency. Likewise, education develops proficiency, but education also cultivates the *powers of reason and judgment* necessary for the martial artist to discern when, and when not, to use the weapons he has worked so hard to develop.

Training Versus Study— The Student's Responsibility

Throughout this book, I use the terms "training" and "study," with an emphasis on *study*. The terms are not completely synonymous. Training is both physical and mental. It prepares and conditions the body and mind to adapt, overcome, and endure, until eventually the two come together as a unit, working toward a common goal or purpose. But training is only *one component* of martial art "study." Study includes training; indeed, in the martial arts, study without training is simply intellectual pursuit. (The world abounds with those whose only physical conditioning is that of their tongues, for they talk endlessly about every aspect of the martial arts—"talking the talk," without ever "walking the walk.")

Study involves sweat; yea, it demands it, for study goes well beyond simple training. Study develops and matures the emotional, intellectual, and spiritual dimensions of the martial artist. This raises the question, "What does the martial artist *study?*" As part of the mind-body pursuit, martial art study should include an investigation of other arts, even if only through review of available literature. You can spend a lifetime mastering one art, so finding time to train and study in more than one is difficult, but you should at least make time to read about other arts. How else can you comment intelligently on such things as why aikido's founder, Morihei Ueshiba, felt that aikido is an "art of reconciliation?" After reading about *aikido* and its founder, you might conclude that the reason Ueshiba made such statements was that he was an already highly skilled and accomplished martial artist. As such, it was easy for him to advocate nonviolence, because he did so from a position of considerable strength. Now, whether or not you agree with this conclusion is unimportant here. The point is that you should attempt to learn something about other arts, their histories, and their founders.

Cultural Understanding

High on the list of things the serious martial artist explores as part of his study is the cultural background of the martial arts. Cultural study of any kind benefits us in many ways: it opens our minds to different ways of thinking and broadens our view of the world. But this "cultural study" is neither immersion into another culture out of some academic motivation, nor is it an exercise in self-improvement. Rather, it is pragmatic recognition of the fact that knowing something of an art's cultural roots is key to understanding that art's fighting techniques. Moreover, since we do not train to fight only those skilled in our art, knowledge of other arts is equally important.

Given that few of us have the opportunity to study and train in the East for a period of time sufficient to absorb the culture, one way to learn something about the culture that spawned an art is by studying its traditions. A martial art's traditions and practices are very often external manifestations of that art's cultural roots. They offer us, therefore, insight into the parent culture. But there are still other reasons why, as a martial artist, you should know more about martial art traditions—even if you do not buy into them all.

Since practically every Asian art has some traditions, it is important to at least understand them, because one way or another, the culture— through the traditions —*will* influence both your study and, in the long term, your life. Whether you welcome this influence or oppose it, your ability to accept or reject it intelligently and successfully is directly related to the degree to which you understand it. Welcoming martial traditions without some understanding of their origins and purpose, can, to put it kindly, make the practitioner appear completely out of touch with reality. Rejecting traditions without a similar understanding displays gross ignorance. Allow me to illustrate.

The student of a Japanese art who abuses the word *ose,* (sounds like ghost) does not fully understand the word, either literally or figuratively. *Ose* is a Japanese word of many meanings, but it is most often used in response to the word, command, or instruction of an honorable person. However, I heard it used at dinner after a seminar when everything the guest teacher said was answered by more than one participant with, *"Ose"* (as though it were an *Amen*). In the United States Marine Corps, the appropriate response to an order is an "aye, aye sir," but outside that environment such a response is completely inappropriate. This is a small linguistic matter, I know, but it exemplifies the type of situation where better knowledge of culture and tradition is helpful.

Cultural and traditional knowledge are also important if the martial artist expects to grow in a variety of arts. For example, in Indonesia, some teachers traditionally ask prospective students if they wish to train with them. There, petitioning the teacher is considered by them to be in poor taste. Many Chinese teachers, on the other hand, would not consider asking even the most talented and promising young man if he would like to train with them. There, the prospective student is expected to petition the teacher continually and persistently, proving his humility, dedication, and worthiness by his importunity. Beyond this, there are still other cultures where formal letters of introduction are required. Without them, one is treated politely, but is also told (politely) to "get lost." This is not to say that one tradition or another is good or bad, or any better or worse than another—just different. Ignorance of another culture, then, can cost you a valuable training opportunity.

Knowledge of the various cultural and martial traditions is also important if you wish to avoid offense. How many students at seminars stand before the guest instructor with their arms crossed in front of them? In many cultures this is a sign of disrespect. Graciously, most Asian seminar teachers assume the student is ignorant of the significance of his action, but their noting it in the first place indicates that it bothers them nonetheless. Some may rightfully argue that the individuals in question are in this country now, and "when in Rome" (or America), they (the seminar instructors) should "do as the Romans do." I cannot fault anyone for feeling this way. I have often felt exactly that way myself. But consider this. The mature martial artist makes every attempt to live in harmony with all those around him, and if a little knowledge and courtesy avert offense, then the martial artist should be the first one in line to demonstrate both. Besides, you will probably learn much more from someone who enjoys you as a student than from someone who is offended (though tolerant).

Applying all this to the "care and feeding" of American martial artists means actively requiring the student to seek knowledge of other arts and their cultural origins, outside his own school. Maintaining a school martial art library is an excellent way to begin. As part of our training program, and beginning with the second belt, each student is required to research and report on various martial arts: Japanese, Okinawan, Korean, Chinese, Filipino, Indonesian, and so on.[1] Information for these papers can be obtained from various public and academic libraries, as well as through personal interviews with teachers of different arts. We do this to see that the student becomes knowledgeable in the origins of, philosophies of, and similarities and differences between the various systems, styles, and arts. Such exposure of students to other arts is a practice that some instructors might find threatening, for fear that they might lose a student to another school (an understandable concern for one who makes his living teaching martial arts). However, the rationale should be that if any student would be happier in another school, studying another art, then he or she should pursue that art.

More important, the exposure to other arts encourages the student to be open-minded and learn—as Dan Inosanto says, "to absorb what is useful." Should the student be interested in competitive events, such exposure prepares him for the day when he, as a black belt, is asked to judge or officiate at tournament. Too many new black belts are uncomfortable the first time they judge a competition, simply because they are unfamiliar with what they are looking at and what they are supposed to be looking for. As a tournament judge, you need not be familiar with a particular pattern or form in another art or system, but you should know something of what an art teaches and why. Such knowledge better qualifies the individual to evaluate the competitors' performance.

Knowing what an art teaches means being familiar with some of the differences in stances between this art and that. For example, in each of the major arts or styles a forward or front stance has some subtle, and some not-so-subtle, differences in both posture and use. The same variation from system to system also manifests itself in the way the blocks and strikes are used and delivered. Knowledge of these differences is indispensable when judging competition (not to mention in evaluating other arts for the purpose of *absorbing what is useful*).

Questionable Traditions

I would be lying to you and untrue to myself if I stopped here. This chapter's third paragraph opens with the statement, "Of all the Eastern martial art traditions, the most valuable ones relate to character development." The statement implies that there are *other-than-best* traditions inherent in Eastern martial arts as well. Does this implication mean that I feel that there are traditions we should do away with? Simply put, yes—at least, they should be modified, either in practice, meaning, or explanation.

Martial artists are some of the busiest people in the world. Most of us spend many hours working a full-time job or profession or receiving an education. Some do both. Add to this load familial obligations, and it surprises me how many of us still find time to train. The stress and requirements placed on us by today's "leaner and meaner" work environment makes training even more difficult. America, I am afraid, is going the way of Japan in this regard. By this I mean that in Japan, martial art study and training appear to be on the decline. Heavy work responsibilities take such a huge chunk out of the individual's day that few are willing to dedicate what free time they have left to such a demanding mistress. So, how does the martial art instructor or school help remedy this? How can we help those wanting to study martial arts make the most of their limited training time—getting the most bang for their bucks?

Language Studies

Long ago, Ed Parker did what was, up to that time, unthinkable. He decided to teach using the host country's common tongue (in the United States, this means English). His bold innovations and insights into the American psyche made his system of American kenpo an instant hit with self-defense enthusiasts everywhere. (It also made him anathema to more than a few classical teachers.)

For those interested in learning another language and culture, martial art study provides an excellent opportunity. Also, for those interested in international competition, learning a common vocabulary makes sense.

But for the busy American student, using English terminology makes more sense. The following analogy illustrates my point.

Recall what it was like when you learned to drive a car. Imagine, now, that your parents had a Volkswagen (for some, imagination here is really unnecessary). Now imagine that you are required to learn the names of all of the components in your automobile in German (a Volkswagen is, after all, a German car). Your driving instructor will also be using German terms, as will the examiner who will test you when you apply for your license. As if that were not enough, you will also have to memorize these terms and use them when you teach others to drive. Terms like, *gaspedal, kupplung, bremse, blinker, lenkrad, schaltknhppel.*[3] Such a challenge might be interesting and even educational; however, it will do nothing to help you learn to drive the vehicle any sooner or more safely. If anything, it will slow your progress considerably.

Likewise, learning a martial art while having to learn a foreign language slows, rather than simplifies, the student's progress. I am not advocating condensed or accelerated training—far from it. However, I remain steadfastly in favor of making the most of our increasingly limited and valuable training time. If you (as a student) are paying for martial art instruction, then you deserve "martial art instruction." If you want foreign language instruction, you can get that elsewhere. Language studies are actually better pursued elsewhere—at a college, university, or with a private tutor. There, much more than just the smallest subset of the language is taught. And in reality, most of the language skills we acquire in the typical karate school will do little to help us locate a telephone, restaurant, hotel, a bathroom, or emergency assistance in the country of origin anyway; and the possibility of engaging in meaningful conversation is even more remote.

FIGURE 5–2

Finally, since all languages have nuances and shades of meaning, concepts transmitted in a foreign language can easily remain hidden to the student. Some might argue that the martial artist should study and pursue the deeper meaning of the new (foreign) terms, but within the context of maximizing training time, this argument is counterproductive. Also, the student is much less likely to receive correct coaching in grammar, usage, and pronunciation when learning from someone other than a qualified language instructor—even if he calls himself "master." How often have I mispronounced this word or that, only to learn the correct pronunciation later and think how dumb I must have sounded.

But school language is only one questionable tradition. Its biggest failing is that it draws from our already limited training time. There are, however, traditions that are questionable for other less obvious reasons. Consider, for example, the practice of bowing.

Bowing

In many schools, students and instructors alike bow before entering or leaving the training area. This is usually done as a sign of respect for a place of learning. In most schools, the students and instructors bow to each other as a sign of mutual respect. In some schools, there is even bowing before the American flag and often before the flag of the country from which the art or instructor came as well. Finally, there are a few schools where it is customary to bow before a school shrine or altar. For a number of Western students, some of these practices are offensive. For a few, they are expressly prohibited.

Mutual Respect

Bowing is not foreign to Western culture. Historically, bowing has been used to demonstrate an attitude of respect, reverence, submission, salutation, recognition, and worship. Bowing as a sign of mutual respect has been practiced in the West for centuries. European gentlemen bowed to each other this way. Moreover, even in Western countries, bowing before a monarch is a required sign of courtesy, respect for, or submission to, regal authority. In the United States, bowing is rather uncommon today, but respect is still displayed. Men, for example, remove their hats when entering a courtroom, and everyone rises when the judge enters. We also rise when our president enters the room or when our national anthem is played. Before the feminist movement, men generally rose when a lady entered the room as well. All of these are signs of respect.

Bowing to fellow practitioners as a sign of *mutual* respect (and I stress the word "mutual") is an acceptable martial art tradition for two of reasons. First, because bowing to our fellows—both juniors and seniors—acknowledges our bond as brothers in the art. Ours is a difficult and challenging path, and one that very few choose to follow. Those who do deserve our respect. Doubtless we will not always like our fellow travelers, but we must acknowledge their dedication to the arts we both love.

The second reason may sound a bit primal, but it is a fact that fighting invariably bonds us together (at least it does the masculine gender). Be it schoolyard fisticuffs or actual wartime combat, whether fighting for the same cause or fighting against each other, respect and friendship often grow from the experience. For example, most men can remember fighting this kid or that in school. Most can recall every significant "battle." Curiously, win or lose, more often than not the combatants came away with more respect for the other than when they began. Often friendships grew from this fertile ground of mutual respect. And this bonding doesn't appear to diminish with age.

Those who have survived the brutality of war often describe similar experiences (the higher stakes only increase the bond). Combat often breeds both lifelong friendship and respect: friendship for our compatriots and respect (albeit grudgingly) for our enemies. Our training in martial arts—because they are martial—falls somewhere between these childhood and actual combat experiences. Whether we are pushing ourselves to our physical and mental limits, testing each other, or helping fellow students to achieve their best, bowing in mutual respect seems a natural extension of this almost primal bond, and one that in martial art training occurs without anyone ever having to become your enemy.

My Master?

As fellow students of the art we bow to each other. As students it is also reasonable for us to bow to our teachers. In so doing we acknowledge their skill and mastery of the art that they share with us. But here again, the act is mutual—the teacher *also* bows to the student. "What?! Bow to my students?" the martial art instructor might ask. Absolutely.

Historically, in the East students often had to petition the teacher simply for the privilege of training with him. They had to prove their worthiness to become pupils. In some cultures this is still the case. However, in the United States, students do not normally petition martial art instructors for long periods of time, seeking admission into their schools. Teaching to make a living has pretty well eliminated this practice. Since there is, therefore, mutual need—the teacher needs students as much as students desire to learn—shouldn't the respect, likewise, be mutual?

Some, it seems, don't think so, for too many instructors still behave as if their skill in martial arts grants them special status. This kind of thinking is flawed, however, because mastery over an individual in the field of

FIGURE 5–3   Bowing before the instructor.

martial arts in no way presupposes mastery in all or any of the other areas of life. (In fairness, I have witnessed this behavior more from culturally American "masters" than I have from Asian ones.) I know, for example, one American instructor who demands that his students call him "MASTER So-n-so." Even his students' parents refer to him as "MASTER So-n-so." (The emphasis on the "master" here is not mine, but the students' and their parents.) I'm not just talking about their calling him "master" in the school. No these folks are conditioned to speak of him as "master" and to introduce him as such to their friends—wherever they may happen to be.

A good friend of mine and fellow martial artist also refers to his teacher (an Asian instructor) as "my master." My friend is a practicing attorney with a doctorate in law. He has worked as long and as hard for his degrees in law as "his master" has for his martial art credentials, yet to my knowledge no one calls my friend "master." His employees don't, his children don't, and I'll wager that his wife wouldn't be caught dead calling him "my master" either. It is incredible to me that Americans, whose forefathers fought for independence, emancipation, and equality, so willingly acknowledge anyone as their master.

The teacher who demands that his students address him as master or bow to him as one who is their master goes too far. Such traditions neither demonstrate nor breed positive character traits—least of all, humility. On the other hand, the teacher who bows to his students in mutual respect recognizes and acknowledges the fact that his students honor him by choosing to train and study in his school. (They can just as easily train elsewhere.) Mutual need, mutual desire, and mutual respect: These should set the tone and spirit for following this traditional Eastern practice. Not some imagined superiority.

Bowing Before National Ensigns

Bowing before the American flag is an acceptable practice because it shows respect for and submission to national authority—authority that (in our country) "we the people" have granted to our government on our behalf. In the past, respect for our flag was something everyone was taught to show.

Beginning in elementary school, we were taught our pledge of allegiance and the words to our national anthem. At the playing of our national anthem, we would stand, place our hands over our hearts, and face our flag. This we did as a sign of respect, allegiance, and rightful submission to the nation our flag so proudly represents. Sadly, this kind of training seems to be lacking today, for fewer and fewer young people demonstrate either the knowledge of this practice or the willingness to embrace it. Bowing before our national ensign, then, is a welcome tradition. Granted, it's not exactly the same as standing with one's hand over one's heart, but the position here is less important than the purpose. However, bowing before another nation's flag, even if out of respect for the nation that now shares her national arts with us, raises some interesting questions.

So we bow before the American flag for the reasons stated, but do we bow before, say, the Korean flag with the same intent: respect, submission, and allegiance? Respect, perhaps, but submission and allegiance? No.

FIGURE 5–4   Bowing before national flags.

Respect for our own country and submission to the leaders we elect to govern us is one tradition we willingly accept—we should, we fought for it. However, it is inappropriate for us to rise and stand with our hands over our hearts in respect for the Korean flag or any other ensign. We might stand, perhaps—out of courtesy and to show no disrespect—but not with our hands over our hearts, which goes a step further to symbolize allegiance.

Likewise, *bowing* which signifies either submission or allegiance is inappropriate. Bowing from any position—seated, kneeling, prone, or standing—goes beyond merely showing respect for it suggests subordination, obeisance, or homage. For this reason, I find bowing before another nation's ensign more objectionable than bowing before my fellow man.

Bowing Before the School Shrine

Followers of some religions and faiths see bowing before a school altar or shrine as an act of obeisance or homage to some spiritual leader or guide. For the practicing Muslim, Jew, or Christian, such a practice is forbidden. For these students training in a school where bowing before a shrine is required, while abstaining from what is, for them, a prohibited practice might subject them to peer pressure to conform or comply. Case in point: one student in an aikido school assumed that bowing before the school altar (one that had an individual's picture on it) was simply an act of respect for the teacher's teacher. This was not particularly troubling to him, so he went along with it. Later, he found out that the individual's picture on the altar was his instructor's spiritual teacher, the Reverend Sun Myung Moon, the founder and supposed "real Messiah" of the Unification Church. In the student's eyes, this was intolerable!

To the *non*-practicing Muslim, Jew, or Christian, these Asian martial art traditions may seem insignificant, but the instructor of any school should be aware of any potential for offense in the traditional Eastern practices he incorporates as part of his curriculum or identity. If Western students are expected to make every effort to understand Eastern culture and tradition, it seems only reasonable that teachers of Eastern arts do likewise.

After saying all of this, I still disagree with those who would ban all traditional Eastern practices from our martial art study. There are ways to balance both Eastern tradition and Western culture. For example, in our school we bow as part of starting and ending class. Like many of the more informal Chinese salutations, our bow is a standing salute. It is not a bow of submission, obeisance, or homage. Rather, it is like an officer returning the salute of enlisted men. With the words "Attention" and "Salute," the teacher shows his respect for his students—they honor him by choosing to study and train with him. The students, in return, echo their respect for the teacher as a worthy instructor and fellow student himself. It is, quite simply, mutual respect. In this way we maintain a tie with our arts' Asian roots, while adapting it to the culture in which we live.

FIGURE 5–5   Bowing before the school shrine.

Abandon Them All?

In this chapter I have pointed out several traditions we should maintain, one that we should eliminate, and one that needs to be considered carefully. We see that where no traditions exist, others spring up and fill the void. Inevitably, the new practices that spring up eventually become traditions. As such, they may be good, or they may turn out to be bad. Sadly, Western experience in this area has not been good.

The traditions found in Western boxing and wrestling (at least in the professional ranks) are negative, rather than positive. These "arts" do not build character, they destroy it. With this experience so close to home, it is the irresponsible instructor who leaves character building to chance. We cannot excuse ourselves with "I only taught my student how to hurt someone. What he does with the skills that I gave him is not my concern." A trainer might say that, but a never a teacher.

Martial art instructors must be more than just trainers and coaches; we must be teachers and educators. Without spending a lot of time indoctrinating our students in another cultural life-style, culturally American instructors are obligated to give their students what the majority of them are asking for (and paying for)—good martial art skills. But we must also equip them with the skills necessary for developing their powers of reason and judgment—skills that prepare them for life as mature martial artists and contributing members of society.

SIX

From Philosophical
to Practical

In karate there comes a time when the orderly progression of
study brings you to the highest level—to spontaneity. You practice basic drills so that you can escape them. As you progress
in the orderly practice of basics, and providing you stay with it
long enough, one day you escape the practice and become
spontaneous.

> —George Anderson, 1992
> (paraphrased)
> *Karate Kung-Fu Illustrated*

The preceding chapters addressed changes in our thinking—changes
necessary for teaching Eastern martial arts to Western students in
general and Americans in particular. This chapter moves from the
philosophical to the practical by recommending simple but fundamental
changes in training methods and practices. Warning: these recommenda-
tions are not for the traditionally faint of heart.

QWERTY

Repetition and practice are, as George Anderson accurately observed (Beaver
1992,20), the keys that unlock the door to spontaneity. However, for spon-

taneity to be effective, those things that are repeated and practiced must themselves be based on sound principles. For example, practicing keyboard skills regularly will make you a better typist. Dedicated practice will make your fingers virtually fly across the keyboard. However, the standard keyboard arrangement—nicknamed QWERTY, for the first six letters on the top alphabetic row—was actually designed to slow the typist.

Type levers on early mechanical typewriters jammed with greater frequency as typists became faster. The QWERTY key layout solved this problem by placing the letters that occur most frequently (in the English language) in the most inaccessible positions. This resolved the problem of malfunctioning typewriters, but it did so at the expense of efficiency.

Over time, mechanical typewriters improved. In the 1930s, electric typewriters appeared; in the 1960s, some machine designs replaced the

FIGURE 6–1   The QWERTY keyboard.

type levers with a type-surfaced ball that moved across the paper (rather than moving the paper under the type). Newer typewriters have now replaced the type-ball with a plastic daisy wheel. Despite these evolutionary advances in typewriter design and capability, one essential element remains unchanged: the QWERTY keyboard.

A more efficient keyboard arrangement was devised in 1936 by August Dvorak. With the Dvorak keyboard, the letters are arranged so that 70 percent of the typing takes place on the "home row." This and other Dvorak improvements mean that a skilled Dvorak typist can type at better than twice the speed of the best QWERTY typist. The Dvorak typist is more productive, not because he or she practices longer than the QWERTY-trained typist, but because the Dvorak keyboard is *based on sound principles* of keyboard design.

The QWERTY illustration exemplifies this chapter's underlying principle: *"Repetition and practice are the keys that unlock the door to spontaneity. However, for spontaneity to be effective, those things that are repeated and practiced must themselves be based on sound principles."* With this maxim in mind, let's look at our first example of classical training and one that is as fundamental to martial arts as keyboards are to typewriters: namely, punching and blocking.

Punching and Blocking Theory

Early in my training I observed that the greatest weakness in classical Asian martial arts is the way they teach basic punches and blocks. Most Asian martial art systems *teach* students to punch and block by extending the punching or blocking arm to the target while simultaneously cocking the other arm at the hip or side (figures 6–2 and 6–3). I emphasize the word "teach" here because experience shows that what is taught, and what students of Asian arts actually use when fighting, are two very different things.

Classical Punching

The theory behind this classical punching method is that it teaches the student the action-reaction principle as it is applied in punching dynamics.

FIGURE 6–2   Classical punching method.

FIGURE 6–3   Counter-hand chambered at the hip.

That is, as he punches or blocks with one hand, he retracts the other hand to the hip, thereby using the hips to develop torque and generate power.

There is no disputing the power claims made by proponents of the classical method. Indeed, coupled with proper hip rotation, punches delivered this way are powerful. However, punches fired from the hip, though powerful, are simply too slow. This is because they have too great a distance to cover before reaching the target. Here's what I mean. Given equal speed, which punch will hit its target first: the one traveling the thirty-five or thirty-six inches from the hip to the opponent's face (figure 6–4), or the one traveling twenty-five inches (figure 6–5)? The answer is obvious.

Before anyone jumps higher than his blood pressure and begins shouting how much more powerful the thirty-five-inch punch is than the twenty-

FIGURE 6–4   36 inches to the target.

FIGURE 6–5   25 inches to the target.

five-incher, consider this: with proper hip and shoulder rotation (shoulder rotation in punching is not usually emphasized in the more popular Asian martial arts), even an eighteen-inch punch will put a man down decisively. They do this in boxing all the time—and with gloves on, no less. But evaluating the effectiveness of punching methods involves another factor: the targets.

Long-armed, thirty-inch-plus corkscrew punches were designed to smash through rigid body armor—and they did their jobs well. Fortunately for the student training to survive in today's environment, his foes are not clad in rigid armor (kevlar, perhaps, but not sixteenth century Japanese *toshi-gusoku* armor). Knowing that your classical punches can "crack the turtle's shell"[1] is comforting only until you run into an opponent who is skilled enough to avoid them.

Beyond the lack-of-speed problem, the classical punching method has another disadvantage: vulnerability. Punching with the counter hand chambered at the hip not only slows your punch (because of its distance from the target), it also creates a mammoth opening in your defense. An opening of this magnitude gives your adversary easy access to such prime targets as your ribs, solar plexus, and sternum. Even if you accept the fact that classical punches are stronger, more power at the expense of one's ribs seems a very poor trade. The classical long-armed corkscrew punch may work well against a board or brick or an unskilled opponent, but against today's quicker, better-trained fighters, it fails—painfully.

Classical Blocking

Classical blocks suffer from the same problems that plague classical punches. Like the punching method, the classical blocking method—with the counter hand chambered at the hip and far from the action—takes much too long to come into play. Further, this slowness is compounded by two other factors: windup and tension. With the classical block, a windup precedes the actual block (figures 6–6 and 6–7). Add to this the fact that the classical block is usually taught with a tightly clenched fist, and you have one very strong arm making an even slower block.

One writer favoring the classical method, suggested that if your block fails to do the job of saving your face, then perhaps the problem is not with the effectiveness of the technique but with your execution or timing of the movement (Lowry 1992, 108). As justification for this position he recounted how some master during World War II dispatched an attacker with a block so powerful that it literally bowled over his hapless assailant.

I cannot dispute the truth of his tale since I was not there to witness the event (and neither was the writer). Moreover, his account of the incident does not include any relevant specifics and circumstances of the attack. (In fairness, the writer would have been hard pressed to share this information in his short column. Nevertheless, we are still left without any hint, for example, of how skilled the master's assailant was, how large or small he was, or any other circumstances that might explain the reported outcome.)

FIGURE 6–6   Classical block—the windup.

FIGURE 6–7   The left arm blocking.

Further, even if the story is true, for every account of one *master's* success, there are dozens of other real-life reports of dismal failure. What is even more surprising is that many examples of this kind of "loss of face" come from the experiences of black belts who have had their clocks cleaned by students of Western boxing. Doubtless, some defenses do fail because of poor execution, but an overwhelming number of them fail because the underlying theory, like the QWERTY keyboard arrangement, is flawed.

I am not particularly a fan of full-contact karate or kickboxing, but when was the last time a full-contact champion used traditional blocks or punches with any degree of success? I can't remember even one. Nor are we witnessing any movement in those circles toward bringing the classical method into the ring. The reason for this reluctance is that today's full-

contact fighters throw devastating, lightning-fast punches from a distance of less than two feet. Against this kind of speed, classical blocks and punches simply do not stand a chance. What amazes me is how a flaw of this magnitude—and one that is taught to thousands of unknowing students every day—still exists in what are, otherwise, extremely potent arts.

FIGURE 6–8   Kickboxing.

Hand Skills—Karate Vs. Boxing

In classical karate, the punches—fired from the hips—are long, and the blocking philosophy is based primarily on deflecting and redirecting the assailant's attack. In boxing, the punches—coming from the shoulder—are shorter, and the blocking philosophy is largely one of absorbing the opponent's blows, usually by taking them on the arms.[2] On the surface, against skilled opponents, boxing hand skills appear superior to those found in classical Asian arts, and from a strictly striking perspective, they are. Boxing has a limited, but highly refined and very effective suite of punching techniques and tactics. However, from an overall self-defense perspective, boxing's blocking methods are limited and otherwise impractical for all but a handful of young, hardened practitioners.[3]

The problem is that, although boxing is excellent for self-defense, it is practiced largely as sport, and its sport trappings are what detract from its combat effectiveness. The biggest of these detractions is the use of padded gloves. This is significant because, from a blocking perspective, the desirability of absorbing punches on the arms evaporates once the gloves are removed. Replacing outdated classical Asian blocking methods with those from Western boxing is, for most of us, then, not the answer. But if not the Western boxer's methods, whose? There is, yet, another option.

Another Option

One of the best punching and blocking systems still comes from Asia: Southeast Asia. Rather than strength and power, speed and mobility are used to the fighter's advantage. In Thailand, Malaysia, Indonesia, and the Philippines, blocking methods evolved differently. Practitioners there rarely use a single strong-arm to block an incoming punch or kick. Instead, they use lightning-fast *multihand* combination blocks and strikes.

Multihand[4] combination blocks and strikes provide better protection from the initial assault because, as with the Western boxing method, both hands are kept between the practitioner and his opponent. However, unlike the boxer's technique, multihand combinations—reflecting their Asian origins—rely on deflection rather than absorption to neutralize the attack.

When intercepting incoming blows, the defender utilizing multihand combinations keeps his hands open, relaxed, and constantly in the field of play. This, coupled with the fact that his hands do not chamber before blocking or striking, means that the hands are much, much quicker to their targets.

It is important to remember here that the benefits of this method exceed those promised by the classical method because multihand combination blocks and strikes are based on sound principles. Equally important, as you will see, is the fact that these combinations are executed exactly as they are practiced. And, as if adding icing to the cake, their practice is both challenging and enjoyable. The following fictitious conversation between the sage martial art teacher and his American pupil illustrates why that last point is important.

> TEACHER: Continue practicing. Remember, it is written that nothing that is worth anything is ever easy.
> PUPIL: Yes teacher. But is it also written that the practice must be so boring?

Serious Fun?

Regardless of the method—Eastern or Western—spontaneous hand reflexes are the result of many hours spent in punching and blocking drills. (There is still no shortcut to spontaneity.) With the classical method you may stand in place practicing the blocks and punches in the air or striking a *makiwara*,[5] march back and forth down the floor doing the same, or work static "one-step" practice sets with a partner. Although these are "time-tested" training techniques, none of them are what you can call challenging or fun.

An alternate method of training, and one that teaches multihand blocks and strikes in a challenging and stimulating way, utilizes a basic two-man drill like the Filipino *hubud*. Parroting the *hubud* drill, multihand training exercises are two-man continuous sets that develop combination-type reactions to an opponent's punches. They develop the skills necessary to thwart a variety of hand attacks. Moreover, they allow both partners to act and react continuously to each other's punches and strikes, developing a flexibility and spontaneity in the practitioners that enables them to adapt to the rapidly changing dynamics of a fight.

The continuous nature of a two-man multihand drill allows both partners to sustain practice for an extended period, thereby accumulating many more repetitions than they would with, for example, any of the traditional methods mentioned above. Nonstop repetition allows each student to monitor and correct his errors with each successive iteration, getting the feel of doing it right. (In this kind of practice, the *feel* of the attack is much more important than the visual perception, because in most real confrontations your ability to see clearly is often reduced.)

As a rule, most *training* methods teach principles of movement rather than actual technique. However, the beauty of the training drill you are about to see—and this is only one of a number of similar drills—is that it does both. It teaches sound principles of movement and, simultaneously, real self-defense technique. As you move through this very basic four-count drill, keep in mind that the first two counts represent the blocking portion and counts three and four the striking part. Although it is possible to separate them, you should do so with care. You see, as a training vehicle, it is the drill's continuous nature that makes the practice of basic blocking and punching fun. Practice that is fun gets more use, and "more use" results in a more effective martial artist. Isolate the components of the drill to understand them, but remember that the real value of the individual components as arranged in this drill lies in their synergistic combination.

A Basic Drill

The drill begins with player-*A* (on the left) executing a right punch to player-*B*'s face. As player-*A* punches, player-*B*'s left hand intercepts *A*'s punch at his hand, wrist, or lower-forearm (figure 6–9) and parries it inward (left-to-right), allowing player-*B* to slip outside *A*'s punch. Player-*B* immediately follows this initial deflection with a second parry that reinforces the first left-to-right movement (figure 6–10). The end of this action has player-*B*'s right forearm sliding alongside his opponent's arm (toward player-*B*). The two motions shown in figures 6–9 and 6–10 make up the blocking portion of the drill. We call this one-two combination or movement, simply, *block-right*.[6]

FIGURE 6–9   Multihand block: left hand intercepts opponent's right punch.

FIGURE 6–10   Right hand, sliding down opponent's arm, reinforces the left to right deflection.

FIGURE 6–11 Clearing (slapping down) opponent's arm.

FIGURE 6–12 Pulling opponent into defender's punch.

Counts one and two are followed immediately by player-*B*'s already positioned left hand slapping down his opponent's right arm (figure 6–11). Some may think that this third count clears or checks player-*A*'s arm, but as you will see, it does much more than that. But let's recap what has just taken place. So far in our drill, player-*A* has punched with his right and player-*B* has responded as follows:

1. Intercepted the punch with a left-to-right left-hand parry (figure 6–9),

2. Reinforced that initial deflection with a second left-to-right right-hand parry that simultaneously slides down his opponent's right forearm (figure 6–10), and

3. Slapped the attacking right arm down with his left hand (figure 6–11).

Figure 6–11 (the third count) begins the striking portion of the drill. The downward slap does, indeed, clear player-*A*'s right arm. More importantly, it also pulls *A*'s face into *B*'s right counterpunch (figure 6–12). Notice that as player-*B* fires off his right punch, player-*A* intercepts it with his left hand, to begin his four-count iteration of the drill.

As a drill, this sequence is routinely practiced in a way that keeps both players *outside* their partners' punches; however, this is not an absolute requirement. It just makes the back-and-forth action of the drill easier to sustain. In reality, the movement is equally effective when applied *inside* a punch, and against either left or right blows. But back for a moment to the third count in this drill: the one that pulls the opponent into the defender's counterpunch.

Some may feel that this multihand method lacks any real power because the hips are not used in delivering the blow. They are partly correct. The hips do not drive the punches. However, the third movement, when executed simultaneously with the fourth (the final strike), actually accelerates the opponent's face into the defender's right punch, resulting in a "head-on" collision of sorts. Does this guarantee a knockout? No, but few punches do.

Even under the best circumstances, the energy you actually transmit to a target with a punch—or any blow for that matter—is always less than optimal, for any number of reasons. This is especially true when striking the head because it is one target that very naturally yields to forces directed against it. Any technique, then, that can simultaneously direct and accelerate this very flexible target into a blow, gains a significant increase in impact. As such, it more than makes up for the lack of hip rotation in its delivery.

The Obvious Obscured

If you examine the multihand block closely, you discover that classical blocks actually spring from the same movement (perhaps hidden by the secretive Chinese merchants when they visited Okinawa). Let's take a close look a classical right outward block as it is taught today. As the block is executed, you find that, although only one arm makes contact with and blocks the incoming punch, the entire movement actually uses *both arms.* Watch.

As the right hand moves right-to-left across your lower torso, the left hand moves inward, across your chest, left-to-right (much like a classical close-to-the-vest left inward block). Some explain this simultaneous movement of the left and right hands as a "windup" for the right outward (left-to-right) block that immediately follows. The *windup* explanation may be

FIGURE 6–13   Classical and multihand blocks—begin.

FIGURE 6–14   Classical and multihand blocks—end.

valid and it is certainly taught this way in many martial art schools, but it looks amazingly similar to the first two counts of the multihand drill. Figures 6–13 and 6–14 provide a comparison.

Is the multihand block an extension of the classical maneuver—or is it the forerunner? The similarities are much too close for mere coincidence. Writer Chris Thomas, in describing the differences in the various Okinawan karate arts, pointed out that one of the obvious changes Chojun Miyagi made in the development of his *goju-ryu* karate was the replacement of many open-hand moves with the closed fist (Thomas 1993, 39). Moreover, he reported that "this tendency to substitute fists for open-hand techniques is a common characteristic of Okinawan karate" and that such changes may have begun with naha-te founder Kanryo Higashionna, himself. If this is the case, then the open-hand method may actually be the predecessor to the clenched-fist method that today we call "classical."

Many arts use open-hand blocks, and an equal number use closed fists; all of them mix both. The point is, we must look for more than just differences in training methods. We must also look for similarities and common principles of movement between arts—regardless of whether they are executed with clenched fists or open hands. Multihand combination blocks work best with *open* hands; however, if their principles are not clearly understood or practitioners simply do not feel comfortable with them, then their evolution to fists with "windups" before execution is understandable. Knowing this, it's possible to see how the practice with fists evolved. But let's continue our examination of the multihand movement and see how it fares against the trained contemporary fighter.

Against a Boxer

The belief that you can fend off a boxer's jab with the classical block, much less stop even a basic one-two punch combination, is wishful thinking. Self-defense martial artists must train realistically and for worst-case scenarios, in training always assume your opponent is a skilled fighter. To assume less is foolish.

Considering the quickness and caliber of the trained boxer—or the seasoned street thug—the multihand, two-man, continuous-action training drill provides the student with defensive tools he can use quickly. That's the beauty of this training method. With just a few hours of practice, even a novice can block and strike with a high probability of success.

I teach these drills to beginning students immediately—before I ever break down the drills into their block-right and block-left[7] movements. You have just seen the drill as practiced against a single punch. It is substantially faster and more effective than the classical method because, as I pointed out before, it keeps both hands between you and your assailant. However, the drill really shines when the skills developed are used against multiple incoming blows—like those you would expect from a boxer (something against which the classical blocking method has some serious shortcomings).

Against a basic left-right, one-two punch combination, the classical outward block might pick up the first punch, but because the defender has his other hand cocked at the hip and far from the action, the boxer stands a much better chance of crashing through with his second shot than the defender does of counterattacking with his own (figures 6–15 and 6–16).

Revisiting the same attack—this time with the defender using the multihand combination—we find the left parry (count one of the drill) intercepting the attacker's left jab—and the right hand that immediately

FIGURE 6–15   Classical block against a boxer.

FIGURE 6–16   The boxer's second strike gets through.

FIGURE 6–17   Multihand block against a boxer.

FIGURE 6–18   Second punch successfully deflected.

follows the left (count two) quickly picking up the attacker's right (figures 6–17 and 6–18).

The multihand approach is not, however, limited to handling only two blows. Since the drills are practiced with the players in constant motion, variables are easily introduced to condition and control the flow. With the hands always in motion, picking up additional punches becomes automatic. (Obviously, you cannot and should not expect to intercept every punch. At some point something other than blocking may be necessary to discourage further attacks.)

If the karate player's *Western nemesis* is the boxer, then these two-man drills are the practitioner's great equalizer. With time and practice, these drills also develop improved hand-eye coordination, quicker reflexes and reaction, better sensitivity to differing degrees of threat, and sophisticated hand skills that are more than a match for a boxer.

◆ ◆ ◆

It is my contention that in the evolution of Asian blocking and striking methods, something was lost. It may have been that Okinawans had different needs, or they lacked an appreciation of the open-hand method (the same might be said of us today). In any case, the result of all this is that many of those still practicing the classical methods do so out of habit, and without a thorough understanding of what they are doing. True to form, they follow the shell of the original movement, but without the substance. Multihand combination blocking, coupled with unchambered punches, returns the substance to a very basic and necessary skill.

Let's now move to what I consider the number two problem in classical Asian martial art training—a problem that goes to the very "sole" of the art: the practice of training in bare feet.

Barefoot Training

Many martial art schools train in bare feet. Why? The answer you hear most often is that it is "traditional." However, this is not entirely correct. The custom is traditional only in some schools. For example, Chinese arts are generally taught and practiced wearing shoes. Most Okinawan, Japanese, and Korean systems, on the other hand, are practiced in bare feet. I say "most" because even among these traditional Asian arts not everyone trains unshod. The Korean art of taekyon, for example, is practiced in shoes.

FIGURE 6–19

77

"Traditional" then, does not mean traditional to *all*, for the custom regarding footwear and martial art training varies widely between arts—even among arts within the same nationality.

Traditional or no, this Eastern custom of training in bare feet is now common practice in many American martial art schools. Throughout the remainder of this chapter we'll examine this custom's unique historical origin and its suitability for us today. Exploring alternatives, we'll look briefly at how martial artists from another part of the world successfully deal with this "thorny" issue. Finally, I will suggest alternative training practices that, based on experience, are better suited to our contemporary American environment.

Why Train in Bare Feet?

In some arts, the reason for barefooted practice is obvious. Schools that teach grappling arts (such as judo, jujutsu, and aikido) need some way to protect the student from injury as he or she is repeatedly thrown to the floor. There, a padded surface protects the student, and bare feet protect the pad. When you consider the fact that few training mats can handle the wear and tear that shoes would inflict on them, the idea of training in bare feet makes sense. "But," you might ask, "what about those arts that don't routinely teach and practice grappling skills? Why do they train in bare feet?" And there is the rub.

Anyone teaching a self-defense art and training in bare feet has to recognize the difference between training without footwear in the school, and real-life survival in the street. This is equally true for all striking arts, not just kicking arts. Proper footwork is critical, even for arts that are primarily hand systems. In martial arts, stability, motion, energy, and power all begin, flow, and end with foot-

FIGURE 6–20   In grappling arts, mats protect the player, and bare feet protect the mat.

work. Whether an art's forté is punching, kicking, or a blend of both, if it claims self-defense effectiveness as one if its goals, and it trains and practices in bare feet, then it has to recognize the contradiction that exists between how it trains and how it expects to fight.

You might, if you really stretch it, raise the same concern over uniforms, noting that, most practitioners and students train in loose-fitting traditional garb. But is there really a tension between this practice, and potential application of martial skills in everyday apparel? Actually, no; for two reasons. First, because the benefit of training in loose-fitting clothes outweighs any lack of reality and, second, because the difference between martial art uniforms and everyday wear is comparatively insignificant.

Training in loose-fitting clothes allows the student to flex and stretch muscles, and thereby exercise through a much greater range of motion than would be possible in a suit or dress—an obvious conditioning benefit. It is true that everyday attire is generally more restrictive than a typical martial art uniform, but kicking to the groin should still be possible even in tight blue jeans. (Anyone whose jeans are so tight that they can't raise their legs that high has a more serious problem than self-defense to deal with anyway.) In reality, any difference that exists between training in a uniform and working in everyday wear, is insignificant when compared to the difference between training-in-bare feet and our modern work-a-day shoe-wearing activities. The uniform question is so weak as to be a nonissue. The next logical question ought to be, "Are there other benefits to barefoot training?" Also, "Are there any disadvantages to training in shoes?" Is it possible that kicking in shoes increases the risk of injury because the shoe is, obviously, harder than an unshod foot? Actually, no.

Medical professionals suggest that the majority of martial-art-related injuries they see are foot and ankle injuries. Although incidents of strained, sprained, jammed, or broken toes makes up a large portion of these numbers, it is estimated that toe injuries are probably many times higher than what is reported. This is because few seek treatment for toe injuries—"after all," they reason, "it's only a toe." (Martial artists are often as long on toughness as they are short on common sense.) Training in shoes reduces these incidents drastically. But since the shoe is, in fact, harder than a bare foot, might we see an increase in other injuries, say, when sparring?

Sparring is a special case, and one that I will address in detail shortly, but for now let me say that for all other types of training—especially since we're not advocating wearing cowboy boots or wingtips—the risk of injury from training in suitable sport shoes is far less than the risks currently realized by training in bare feet. A better question might be, "Are there other benefits to training in bare feet—like conditioning and callousing them?" With the possible exception of sparring, the answer is also, no—unless, of course, you spend most of your waking hours in bare feet. If I've overlooked some obvious benefit to training in bare feet, I apologize, but I see no reason, beyond those already stated, why we in the West should train barefooted. We could rehash this side of the issue forever, but that would put us no nearer the truth. Let's look, instead, at the origins of this now common training custom.

Origins

The origin of barefoot training is interesting. It comes from a culture and period in history when the common man routinely went without shoes. It is not surprising, then, that martial artists of that period, likewise, did not train in shoes. Since their martial skills were primarily for self-defense, those men trained realistically; they trained for the environment in which they lived. This meant training in bare feet. Shoes simply were not an option. (For that matter, neither were safety equipment and groin protection.)

Other cultures and levels of society, although well acquainted with footwear, customarily removed their shoes, for example, when going indoors. Some cultures do this still. If, therefore, the training hall was indoors, then the training was (you guessed it) conducted in bare feet. This is one way *cultural* practices wend their way into martial art training, eventually becoming *martial art* traditions.

Barefoot training, however, in a country and culture where everyone wears shoes and only the smallest minority removes them on going indoors, raises some interesting questions. How do you, for example, curl your toes in a shoe? In a shoe, is the ball of the foot or the blade (the edge of the foot) still the optimal striking surface? How easily is the kick performed in wingtips or cowboy boots? In street shoes, is a heel kick executed with the toes pulled up and with the foot at a right angle to the shin, or are the toes extended?

Having trained in bare feet for more than a decade before switching to training in shoes, I can say unequivocally that training in shoes is as different from training in bare feet as day is from night. Further, curling the toes inside a pair of hard-soled leather shoes is not easy, and I do not recommend

FIGURE 6–21   Sandals lined up outside the dojo door.

even trying to do so. Kicking with the blade of the foot is also a poor idea. Against a hard target, it is a sure ankle buster. Moreover, when executing spinning heel and hook kicks in shoes, the foot and heel are definitely held in a different position (the foot is extended, the toes are pointed, and the strike is routinely made with the bottom of the foot). Training in shoes is, in fact, so different from training in bare feet that most kicking theories fly right out the window. How, then, do we rectify this? How do we train in shoes (for self-defense realism) and, at the same time, retain good form while insuring the safety of all the participants? Where do we begin and what practices must we observe or avoid? Let me show you what works for us.

A Practical, Shoes-On Approach

I joined the United States Marine Corps just eight years after the conclusion of the Korean War. While on active duty, I met many veterans of that "conflict" who fought alongside Turkish units (Turkey was a part of the United Nations force). Without exception, every marine I spoke with acknowledged the toughness and fighting skill of our Turkish allies. This

Is this
Billy Jack?

FIGURE 6–22

was high praise from marines. Well, Turkish commandos (the best of their best) train extensively in Asian fighting arts. Visit their training camps and you will see them practicing many of the same punching and kicking drills we practice here. One thing is different, though—very different: *they train in what they fight in.* They train in combat fatigues and wearing heavy combat boots.

Witness their breaking demonstrations, where commando after commando smashes through stacks of roof tiles and cinder blocks, and you are immediately taken by their dedication and skill. You also notice, just as quickly, their camouflaged fatigues and their tall black combat boots. Turkish commandos have whole-heartedly adopted Asian fighting arts, but, more important, they have just as aggressively adapted them to their specific environment and needs. American martial artists must do the same.

Simulation of Reality

Begin by accepting the fact that all training is based on the *simulation* of reality. The operative word here is simulation. This means that while wingtips and cowboy boots are for many, reality, they are unacceptable for training (unless, of course, you want to wear them as you smash stacks of roof tiles). The civilian martial artist is better off working out in some type of training or exercise shoe. You can use the latest lightweight martial art training shoes advertised in many trade publications, but you should really only use them for a short period—as, say, a transitional step to wearing a better (and yes, heavier and more realistic) training shoe. (Lightweight shoes wear out very quickly under serious training anyway, and they provide little more than minimal toe protection.) The shoes you wear in training should, as closely as possible, approximate the weight and feel of what you wear everyday. It is unlikely that they will be exactly like what everyone is accustomed to, but they should come close (remember, we're talking simulation here).

Moreover, the shoes you wear when training should *not* be worn outdoors. I repeat, they should *not* be worn in the street. A Student may wear everyday shoes to and from the school. However, his or her training shoes are worn *only* in the actual training area. This is critical because clean, in-the-school-only training shoes minimize wear and tear on training equipment such as heavy

FIGURE 6–23   Today's martial artists can choose from a variety of martial art and athletic training shoes.

bags, air shields, and some of the newer (and expensive) training mats. Even ordinary dirt has enough abrasive content to ruin good training equipment, so clean shoes are an absolute requirement.

As a rule, running shoes (those with wedge soles) do not work very well for martial art training because they provide insufficient lateral support. (Try practicing a horse stance in a running or jogging shoe for any length of time and you'll discover that your feet soon slide over the soles as the shoe's upper material stretches.) Cross-training shoes and racquet ball shoes work very well, however. As recreational, sport, and athletic shoes continue to evolve, better ones are sure to appear, so keep looking for the best shoe for you. It may be developed for another sport, but still be well-suited for your training.

Not to be forgotten are the medical reasons for training in shoes: good shoes greatly reduce wear and tear on the student. All-out "blitz" training (that is, practicing techniques that require an explosion out of the gate) and hard-hitting back and side kicks on a heavy bag are extremely stressful on the foot, knee, hip, and spine. Recognizing these hazards, martial artists have for years sought ways to prolong training without wearing out their bodies. However, some of the solutions devised for this problem are absurd. For example, some schools install specially designed floors to reduce impact-related foot stress and strain (Lowry 1993, 126). (One school

OK. Whatcha gonna do now?

FIGURE 6–24

even installed thousands of small springs under the wood flooring!) All of this so that they can continue to train the traditional way. The motivation here is admirable, but the method is extreme. Altering the training surface to reduce or prevent barefoot-training injuries makes about as much sense as softening the highways to smooth the ride for automobiles, trucks, and buses. Isn't this why automobile and tire manufacturers designed low-pressure rubber tires and fluid and gas shock absorbers? Instead of making the floor softer, isn't it smarter to simply have everyone wear clean, quality workout shoes? Certainly, it is a whale of a lot cheaper (not to mention warmer).

Even when students are training on concrete floors (not something I recommend), proper shoes significantly reduce the stress that typical martial art training places on the *all* joints of the body, not just the feet. Slamming the human foot on the floor or into a heavy bag produces, literally, hundreds of pounds of pressure per square inch on the foot. The shock from this force is transmitted through all of the joints involved. Good training shoes provide a cushion for the heel and the ball of the foot that the unprotected foot does not naturally have. As such, they dramatically reduce physical wear and tear. Good training shoes, then, are a must for training longevity. (And think about it: the longer you can train, the better you can be.) That said, there remain some situations where training in shoes may be impractical.

Sparring Anyone?

I pointed out earlier that for martial artists studying grappling arts, barefoot training is necessary to protect both the student and the training surface. Shoes should not be worn there—for now. When the day comes that reasonably priced padded surfaces can handle the wear and tear of training shoes, then the issue of training shoes and grappling arts should be revisited.[8] But what about other arts—like stand-up striking arts? Are there times when their practitioners should not wear shoes? You bet.

As a rule, training in shoes is an excellent idea. However, wearing shoes during sparring is taking a good idea too far. To protect all the players, commercial safety equipment specifically designed for sparring, should be used— not training shoes. "Aha," you might say, "doesn't routinely training in shoes leave your feet unprepared for sparring? Won't your uncalloused feet be too tender to take the abuse that sparring on a hardwood floor places on them?" You are absolutely correct. My feet are too tender for sparring on a hardwood floor (or a carpeted one for that matter), but there is a very simple solution. When sparring, wear socks and *soft leather gymnastics slippers* under your safety footgear. The socks and soft leather protect the feet very well—and without the risk of injury to your sparring partner. We wear gymnastics slippers and thick socks under our padded footgear and routinely spar for an hour or more on a very abrasive carpet with not so much as a blister. This effectively eliminates the need to condition the feet by training in bare feet. (If it sounds like I am hammering away on this issue, I am. You would be surprised at the lengths to which some go to maintain even a bad status quo.)

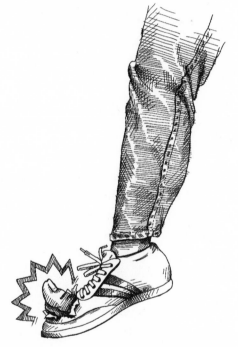

FIGURE 6–25   Curling the toes in shoes has its problems.

Surprisingly, even without the weight of a real shoe, most of the footgear commonly available gives the student almost the same feel as everyday shoes. For example, I remember when commercially produced foam-dipped modern safety gear first appeared. Everyone howled about how they felt like they were fighting with watermelons on their feet. Not surprisingly, it dawned on very few of us (myself included) that we would feel just as uncomfortable (and probably more so) having to kick while wearing regular street shoes. Wearing lightweight sparring footgear simulates very well the feeling of *fighting in real shoes*—and without the risks inherent in actually sparring in them. Used together, training shoes and the padded sparring footwear *simulate* reality very well. Remember, fighter pilots spend countless hours training in flight and combat simulators. Every effort is made to make their training as real as possible. Shouldn't we do the same in our training?

Changing Paradigm

Paradigm is a word we hear a great deal today, as in "the changing paradigm." By definition, a paradigm is *an example or pattern, an outstandingly clear model from which all things of the same type are represented or copied.* An example of a changing paradigm is the Swiss watch. At one time, Swiss watchmakers produced 90 percent of the watches sold in the world. However, when digital watches were introduced, Swiss watchmakers felt that no one would want them, so they continued making traditional analog timepieces (watches with hands that are built using jewels, springs, and gears). This was an unfortunate miscalculation on their part. They did not recognize that the paradigm had changed. The public readily accepted quartz technology and digital watches, and today only 10 percent of the watches in the world are produced in Switzerland. The parallel for martial artists is this: instead of putting our efforts into developing training surfaces that allow us to continue training in bare feet, we should accept the fact that the paradigm has changed and today, in the West, training in bare feet makes no sense.

The commandos I witnessed smashing through roof tiles with their spinning back kicks, hook kicks, and turning round kicks, suffered no lack of proper form, focus, power, or balance. Their combat boots in no way inhibited or diminished their expert execution of the art they practiced. You have to admire their dedication, their skill, and their love of the art. More importantly, you have to admire *their adaptability.* For them, and for us, training in shoes makes perfect sense—both from a practical self-defense side and from a medical/safety one.

Updated Training Methods

The typewriter has come a long way since its debut in 1867. Its longevity is testimony to its usefulness. In our technological society, the typewriter may be replaced by the personal computer, but typewriter keyboards remain, and so does the QWERTY keyboard arrangement. Despite the fact that the limitations responsible for the QWERTY design have long since been overcome, the admittedly inefficient arrangement doggedly remains with us still. This parallels the state of Asian martial art training today.

Martial arts have come a long way since their introduction in the West. Their longevity stands as testimony to their usefulness as systems of self-defense. The difference between martial artists and typists is that typists admit that the old QWERTY keyboard is outdated. Practitioners of classical arts refuse to recognize, much less admit, that some of the things they do are no longer effective. Fighting continues to evolve, but too many martial art teachers steadfastly refuse to free themselves (and their students) from their arts' inefficient and archaic training baggage.

Just as the classical QWERTY keyboard reduces the typist's effectiveness, outdated training methods reduce the effectiveness of once potent Asian fighting arts. Wish as some might, there's no escaping the truth that *what we practice* (in training) *is what we will do* (in a fight). We may practice diligently, eventually escaping the routine and developing spontaneity, but if our efforts are based on unsound and outdated principles, then we make ourselves vulnerable to adversaries with less training but superior methods.

Training methods of the past mirrored the combat environment of that day: the toes were curled and the feet held in specific positions to maximize power and minimize vulnerability. We understand this. However, *the paradigm has changed.* The rules of engagement and the environment are very different today, and classical training methods must change. What we're talking about is much, much more important than the difference between QWERTY and Dvorak keyboards. What we're talking about may be the difference between a student's life and death.

SEVEN

Kata—Forms Training

Kata was designed by warriors who depended upon their skill in the martial arts to stay alive. When a warrior performed a kata, it was for his benefit; each movement practiced was a technique designed to incapacitate his opponent. Individual techniques were performed just as they would be executed in a combat situation.

—Rick Clark, 1989
Inside Karate magazine

Called *kata, kuen,* and *hyung* in Japanese, Chinese, and Korean, respectively, forms are basically choreographed shadow boxing. Largely a solo-practice training method, forms practice can also be done as synchronized or coordinated multiman routines. Practiced with weapons or with empty hand, forms were originally designed to teach technique, movement, and proper breathing, and to develop and condition the body—all of this for self-defense. Today, however, most kata[1] are taught and practiced for very different reasons, leading many in the martial art community to question their value for the contemporary practitioner. This chapter examines forms training and asks the question, *"Is it still a useful training tool?"*

Is It Still a Useful Training Tool?

Over the years my position on kata has changed from one of complete dis-dain to that of conditional appreciation. Accepting that the original pur-pose behind forms training was self-defense, as stated by Rick Clark above (1989, 61), I once believed that if a technique in a form is not performed *exactly* the way it is applied in the street, then it should either be changed or discarded. I realize now, however, that within reasonable limits, it is acceptable to see some deviation between a fighting technique in applica-tion, and how it is executed in kata. This is because the various movements in a form or pattern do more than simply teach self-defense techniques: some build strength, others improve flexibility; still others use repetition to ingrain some basic pattern of movement into the student's mind.

Visualize, for example, a technique where actual application has the defender executing a rising front kick to his assailant's groin (figure 7–1). This same technique is performed in kata (or practice), with the same ris-ing front kick, but in the form the kick may legitimately rise as high as the imaginary opponent's face (figure 7–2). From a self-defense perspective, kicking to the head weakens, rather than strengthens the defender's tech-nique; however, from a training perspective, not only is the high kick accept-able, but, in some ways, it is desirable. When used in self-defense, the tech-nique has *one* and only *one* objective: disabling your opponent. When practiced in a kata, however, its purpose is broadened to serve the follow-ing two additional functions:

- Teaching basic movement
- Physical conditioning

Teaching basic movement is critical, for just as protons and electrons are the building blocks of atoms, movements are the building blocks of techniques. In any fighting technique, a block—any block—is simply a movement. A punch or a kick is another movement. Combine the two, and you have a basic technique. Learn any system, style, or fighting art's movements, and you have all that you need to create your own techniques.

FIGURE 7–1   Front kick in application.   FIGURE 7–2   Front kick during practice.

"Learning an art's movements" involves much more than simply learning to put the hand here or the foot there. It also means developing a thorough understanding of, for example, a movement's purpose, mechanics, and underlying principles. Understanding motion and movement at that level provides you with everything you need to create your own techniques. This is exactly what you do when you move beyond the practice and into the realm of spontaneity: in combat, you spontaneously create your own techniques. Of the two objectives and functions listed for kata, then, *teaching basic movement* is the most important.

Behind teaching practical self-defense and basic movement, physical conditioning is the third purpose of forms training. If, for example, you practice kicking higher than necessary during training (something you do when warmed up and in appropriate, loose fitting, apparel), then you should have little difficulty kicking the lower, more practical targets when in street clothes and with no time to stretch or warm up. Forms training is where we push and extend what are otherwise practical limitations—exaggerating our moves, deepening our stances, and heightening our kicks. These limit-pushing exercises—impractical in a real fight—develop the flexibility, strength, balance and coordination that the fighter needs if he expects to succeed in that real altercation.

Classical Mess

Beyond these three basic functions of kata, there remains a nagging problem. Too many forms today no longer teach relevant, practical self-defense technique, or even the basic movements from which such techniques are built. For those studying an art for reasons other than self-defense this is not a problem, but for those studying an art primarily for self-defense, it is a major one. Attack, defense, and methods of movement continually change. They also differ considerably from culture to culture. Most classical kata represent a method of combat that is radically different from the way we Americans fight today.

In Chapter 4, you were shown an example of a knife technique from the days of the samurai. That technique is vastly different from the fighting methods used by modern knife aficionados; it has to be. Like a knife technique from the past, a *naginata* or halberd a kata from a bygone era will very likely contain techniques and patterns of evasion and movement that are based on the premise that the opponent is, for example, on horseback and carrying a weapon common to that era (but one that is uncommon today), or that he is wearing some type of protective armor. Techniques designed for those circumstances might be completely inappropriate and, therefore, ineffective today. These are major differences that most classical forms do not address. For the most part, then, forms development has not kept pace with the differences and changes in fighting.

Contemporary Mess

Classical forms are not the only culprits in all of this. Many today teach modern forms that have even less (if any) martial application. Tinfoil swords, super-lightweight weapons that break on impact, and weapons that allow you to beat yourself with little fear of raising even a small welt, are not martial art weapons. Practicing kata with toy-like replicas of the real thing is like heading off to the pistol range and whipping out your plastic "Dirty Harry" Smith & Wesson 44. That piece may look impressive, but it is even less than the real thing is when its empty; it lacks real substance.

FIGURE 7–3   Lacking real substance, a plastic gun offers little for self-defense.

I remember a young tournament competitor whose performance in kata was very impressive. It was good that her chronological age confined her to a youth division, because her skill and heart would have humiliated many of the adult black belt competitors.[2] This young lady performed an exquisite *naginata* kata. Not only that, she performed it with a weapon that most male competitors would not care work with. The weapon was heavy and difficult to maneuver; however, because she practiced with this real classical weapon—only the blade was dulled for safety—she developed a real appreciation of the skill necessary to handle such a formidable instrument. She also understood the potential and limitations of the weapon many times better than one training with a lightweight replica. Few competitors today understand their empty hand forms to that extent, let alone their weapons kata.

Unrealistic weapons breed bad habits and a lack of respect for the real thing. Back flips, splits, and "moon walks" now common in so many modern tournament forms may be entertaining, but they are *not* martial art. At best, such moves have only limited, if any, martial application. As outdated and ineffective as some classical forms may be, they are at least based on once-effective self-defense techniques and fighting scenarios.

Numerous problems plague classical and contemporary kata alike. What is needed, then, is a balance between the classical approach and the contemporary, go-for-show artistic license so prevalent today. There needs to be movement back to the *original* purpose of kata: teaching effective self-defense. With that purpose in mind, today's martial artists need to develop new forms—or change existing ones—so that they, once again, contribute to effectiveness in combat.

Understanding Forms Training

Examine kata in light of their original purpose, and you come to the realization that most self-defense forms fall into one of two groups: training forms and demonstration forms. Let's look at the difference between them.

Training Forms

Training forms are usually repetitious and often very basic. They teach the student what I call *movements*. Movements are broken down into *movement* and *motion* (the basic components of fighting techniques)—like learning an alphabet and building a vocabulary. *Movement* involves stances and how to move from position to position smoothly—left, right, off-center, spinning, and so on. *Motion*, on the other hand, is how we strike with our elbows in, say, a half-dozen different ways. Practicing elbow strikes repeatedly in a kata may not be very "pretty." The sequence may not even constitute a practical technique, but practical techniques are only effective when they flow, and they will not flow without sufficient practice. Training forms give the student the basics that are needed for the demonstration forms. (For the remainder of this chapter I will use the term "movements" to mean both movement and motion.)

Demonstration Forms

Like training forms, demonstration forms also teach, but they teach something else. Demonstration forms provide the martial artist with possible sequences for the movements learned earlier in the training forms. Ultimately, demonstration forms should exemplify the practitioner's art, style, and skill—taking the "characters and words" learned in the training forms and making them into intelligible sentences and cohesive paragraphs. That which the martial artist learned in the training forms should be evident in his execution of the demonstration forms, and it is here that the dramatic element is introduced.

The introduction of drama does not mean the excessive snarling, facial expressions, and antics so common today. It does mean adding the intensity, focus, and eye contact between you and your invisible opponent: things like a look of surprise as you duck or leap over his attack. Snarling and other excessive facial displays are merely poor attempts at the higher level of acting skill necessary to make a form come alive. Kata represents the age-old struggle of life and death, of good against evil. That reality is dramatic enough. Adding fantasy only detracts from it. Demonstration forms, then, should be where the individual's style polishes his already excellent technique—not where style overpowers it.

It is unrealistic to believe that a single form can both teach basic movements and provide the student with a substantive demonstration platform. To learn demonstration forms *without* spending sufficient time on the training forms results in, at best, a mechanical copy of the movements. On the other hand, the martial artist who spends sufficient time in training forms develops "flow." Flow is spontaneous, shaping itself dynamically to meet the need. Flow comes only after hours of repetitive practice. Training forms develop this flow. Demonstration forms, on the other hand, show that development. Forms training must teach both: *movements,* to ingrain the desired reflexes, and *techniques* to provide possible sequences for those movements. Done this way, forms practice is a very useful training tool.

Change or Sacrilege?

There are those who call this idea of changing forms sacrilege, asking, "What right do we have to change what many masters have spent their entire lives developing?" What do we say to them? We can answer with the words of a past master who said that his goal was to revise kata . . .

> . . . so as to make them as simple as possible. Times change, the world changes, and obviously the martial arts must change too. The karate that high school students practice today is not the same karate that was practiced even 10 years ago, and it is a long way indeed from the karate I learned . . .

Recognizing that change is inevitable, that same master also said,

> I have no doubt whatsoever that in the future, as times change, again and then again, the kata will [even] be given new names. And that, indeed, is as it should be.

That master was none other than the founder of Shotokan karate himself, Gichin Funakoshi (1981, 36–37).

It takes little research to find master after master who took what his teachers gave him, refined it, and subsequently created a new system. There are past and present masters who can, and do, change and create forms. (I mentioned earlier how Chojun Miyagi changed the forms he brought into his goju-ryu karate from their original open-hand expression to those using fists.) There are also those who, though formally qualified, should *not* do so. The ability to create or modify forms requires more than credentials. Credentials only represent recognition of ability. Knowledge of forms (historically and technically) and the ability to perform them are only part of what it takes to create or change kata.

A bigger part is this, does an individual possess sufficient experience and knowledge in his art to analyze its forms, and where necessary, revise them? Some will disagree and would have us believe that IQs have mysteriously dropped in the last 100 years. They believe that only *past* masters were smart enough and experienced enough to make such changes. Without a doubt, static, unchanging arts make an instructor's life so much easier because they simplify what he must teach. However, such thinking does not face reality. In any art or science today, one is hard-pressed to find a subject that remains static and unchanging.

Change is inevitable. The questions, then, are as follows: Can an individual analyze, adapt, change, and even create forms that are both aesthetically pleasing and technically potent? Do the new forms demonstrate proper speed, power, focus, and flexibility? Do they flow from one technique to another without hesitation? Most important, do the forms prepare one for combat?

All of this in no way means that we ignore or discard the work of past masters.

FIGURE 7–4   Gichin Funakoshi, 1868–1957.

What they passed on to us should serve as a foundation on which we build. We owe them our gratitude and respect. However, we should never so hallow their work that we label it as "perfect" and, therefore, unchangeable. Nor should we consider *our* creations, our new forms, as unchangeable.

Necessary and Natural Change

Dan Inosanto provided an excellent example of necessary and natural change. He pointed out that in track and field record after record falls. Why? Partly because of advances in equipment, but largely because the training methods have been constantly replaced with better ones. Can you imagine a 100-yard dash between a turn-of-the-century Olympian and one from the last Olympiad? There would be no contest! (My only hope would be that the modern Olympian would be as gracious in accepting the win as he was fleet-of-foot in accomplishing it.)

If forms practice is to remain a viable training tool for today's martial artist, it, too, must be allowed to change. Classical kata represent the combat techniques of past masters. Contemporary kata should reflect the combat techniques of our day.

If your goal in martial arts is "cultural study," keeping some time-honored tradition alive, that's OK; just stop calling it a "martial art." Call it "classical" or "traditional _____ martial way" (fill in the blank with the culture of your choice).

If your goal is entertainment, have fun, but do not call that martial art either. Call it martial dance, gym-kata, whatever.

If, on the other hand, you wish to keep alive those things past masters gave their lives for, then do it with the same fire and vision they had. Create a work of art that springs from the very root of martial arts: self-defense. Create a form that represents the combat techniques of your day. Season it with just enough drama to make it come alive and, *voila*! Forms training will be everything it is supposed to be.

Appreciate classical forms as a vital historical link to the past. Learn the principles they teach, because principles of movement remain constant, and these principles spring from the fountain of past experience. Enjoy the entertainment forms for their gymnastic skill and theatrical showmanship. Add some of that drama and visualization to your demonstration forms. Remember, however, that drama and showmanship, like salt and pepper, only please the palate when used in moderation. Too much, and the entrée is not fit for consumption. Finally, balance everything with your personal martial art goals; then, forms practice will be as useful a training tool for you as it was for the masters of the past.

EIGHT

Sport Karate

Sport karate[1] is very popular in the West, and especially in the United States. Not surprisingly, there are as many kinds of sport karate competition as there are misconceptions about it. My purpose in this chapter is to help you see this part of the art for what it *really* is. You may believe, as some do, that sparring and tournament competition are of no real benefit to the martial artist. On the other hand, you may believe that the only real martial artists are those who "put it on the floor," testing it in the ring. Knowing what sport karate really is (or should be) corrects both of these misconceptions and goes a long way toward helping everyone benefit from taking part in it—either as spectators or participants. Let's begin our examination of this most visible aspect of the art at its beginnings.

Owing to the sport's popularity (and our American passion for competition), it is

FIGURE 8–1   Open karate tournament.

COURTESY C. JOHN MACE, 1995

101

easy to see how one might naturally assume that the sporting aspect of these Eastern arts is largely a Western innovation. However, such an assumption is incorrect. The modern karate tournament actually began under the auspices of Shotokan founder Gichin Funakoshi.

Initially, Funakoshi opposed the idea of a karate tournament. His fear was that the rules necessary to make karate safe for tournament play would also dilute the art, eventually rendering it completely ineffective. Convinced by tournament supporters that tournament play would, instead, help spread the art he loved across the globe, Funakoshi acquiesced, and in 1950 the first large-scale karate tournament was held in Japan.[2] Since then, tournament competition and sport karate have taken off, and true to the promises of its proponents, karate is now practiced around the world. But have the great master's fears been assuaged or realized?

The Games Martial Artists Play

Sport karate and tournament play are games played by martial artists to display and test some of their skills. Judo has been played in organized competition for long enough that it enjoys the status of being an Olympic event. Tae kwon do is an Olympic demonstration sport, and karate is working hard to earn a spot on the Olympic roster as well.

FIGURE 8–2   Sport karate: point fighters.

Martial artists interested in sport participation have several avenues they can pursue. There are "traditional" tournaments where only prescribed forms or kata are welcome. Fighting there is tightly controlled, with only the classical techniques being favorably received and scored. These are generally "invitational" or "closed" events that are not open to all styles. These classical or traditional arts are also the ones that are most likely to make it into the Olympics.

At the other end of the spectrum are the

"full-contact" events. There the emphasis is totally on fighting. Within the full-contact group there are organizations that use pads and those that do not. Although a few allow kicks below the belt, most do not. Some even allow grappling and wrestling, but for now, in the West, they are in the minority. In the full-contact arena, kata competition is not a competitive event. There it is relegated to minor demonstrations between the major events—the fights. Between these two extremes are a wide range of tournaments that allow and disallow various techniques.

Is Sport Karate Real Fighting?

How is the martial artist to know which type of competition is for him? How is he to know which of these types of fighting is the most "real?" Actually, none of these events—the ultra-traditional, invitation-only classical tournament; the wild and woolly full-contact bouts; and everything in between—qualifies as "real." All of them are games. Games that can be bloody and brutal, true; but games nonetheless.

I should mention the latest fad in martial sport competition: "no rules" events like the Ultimate Fighting Championships (UFC) started by the Gracies (Brazilian Jiu-jitsu aficionados). They advertize these events as having no rules; however, when pressed for accuracy, they will admit that there are some "restrictions." As good as the Gracies are (and they are very good on the ground), their "NO RULES (but some restrictions)" statement only adds the game of semantics onto their martial game. Such events, while educational for the martial artist, come as close to "real"

FIGURE 8–3   Thai boxers.

103

as you can get, but, in the final analysis, they are still only games. More brutal, perhaps, but still games, with rules.

In reality, there are only degrees or shades of difference between Olympic tae kwon do; AAU karate; full-contact, no-pads karate; kickboxing; and the "no rules" events. The differences are all in the rules. For example, you cannot punch to the head in Olympic tae kwon do; the same is true in practically all full-contact bare-knuckle karate events. Olympic tae kwon do; AAU karate; full-contact, bare-knuckle karate; and kickboxing all disallow groin and leg attacks, and although the "no rules" events allow elbows and ground-fighting, they prohibit biting and eye-gouging (I mean "restrict"). The only American sanctioning body allowing leg kicks today is the World Kickboxing Association. Although the players will disagree, none of these "sports" (including the "no rules" events) can still claim to be real fighting. This is because "real" is a relative term and one delineated only by differences in the rules. All of them, for example, have at least one rule: no weapons. Again, "real" is a relative term.

That said, it is important to realize that these games are not for everyone. They are not even necessary to make one a good martial artist. For example, my current instructor has never fought in a tournament in his life (although he has fought *for* his life on more than one occasion). In more than half a century of training, he has never felt the need to compete. He rarely even participates in public demonstrations. Despite his lack of tournament experience he is, without a doubt, one of the most capable martial artists I have ever come across. One of my best friends, on the other hand, has fought in practically every type of sport-karate event there is: full-contact, point karate, good rules, bad rules; sometimes, what even looked like no rules. My friend has a win/loss record most of us can only wish for. His success speaks for itself. But my friend has not stopped there. He used his sporting interest as a springboard to developing a depth and breadth of skill in the art that few can claim. His sport successes aside, few will argue that he is anything less than a true martial artist possessing knowledge and skills well beyond his sporting abilities.

Looking at the divergent paths of these two men, we can rightfully conclude two things. First, that participation in martial sports is not necessary to be a successful and capable martial artist. Second, that participation in such sport can be an effective vehicle for making one a successful and capable martial artist. This seems to place the competitive aspect of martial arts in the "take it or leave it" category. But deciding to "leave it" may mean missing out on an effective training tool. As martial artists, we are unwise to pass on anything that has the power to make us better.

Water Polo Anyone?

My support for tournaments, both as a competitor and a tournament official, now spans nearly three decades. My involvement as a participant, however, has been limited to point tournaments only (as opposed to full-contact), so I will confine my observations to that arena. I am still active in supporting tournaments that benefit the competitor, but after considerable thought, I have come to the following conclusions. First, tournament play today is rarely held for the benefit of the competitor. Second, although tournament play is only a game, it is still a game that has the *potential* to teach because of its martial roots, emphasis, and application. Today, the push is for tournaments to become exclusively martial *games*, all the while claiming martial roots, but surrendering their martial emphasis and applicability. How has this happened?

Originally, tournaments were held for the martial artist, to afford him a legitimate platform to show his skills and test some of them against new opponents and differing styles. Now, however, tournaments are held for just about everyone else *but* the competitor. A few recognized and respected martial artists, like Bill Wallace, are telling us that, "What we've got to think about is spectator appeal. We have to draw more spectators to the art . . . and the spectators do not want all that violence." (Considering the success of "no rules" events like the UFC, it seems that just the opposite is true.) Any tournament run for "spectator appeal" is obviously *not* being held for the sake of the competitor.

What we are told is that the *public* will not like what attracted us, martial artists, to the art, so we must water it down to a point where they (the

FIGURE 8–4

spectators) will. The result is a premium paid for ineffective technique, like two-point head kicks and three-point jump kicks, while penalizing what is effective (awarding only one point for punches and eliminating attacks to the groin altogether).

This cry for entertainment for the purpose of exposing the art to the public has reduced the art's effectiveness and its respect in the public's eyes. Little wonder many martial artists see no benefit in sport competition. More than a few believe that when it comes to fighting, tournament fighting competition has little value in preparing one for survival in the street. They argue that sport karate has ruined the art by turning once-potent lifesaving skills into little more than water polo. Water polo and lifesaving have many similarities, and one *major* difference. Both occur in the water.[3] Both involve fetching an object. But which expert would you want around if you were drowning?

As a martial artist, I have to agree with much of what tournament detractors say. In a growing number of tournaments, the rules are skewed in favor of flashy, high-kicking techniques—high-risk techniques that, if used in the street, make the kicker extremely vulnerable to a leg kick or groin strike. This is especially true on the national circuit. Nevertheless, I still believe that, given the right environment, competitive events are beneficial for the martial artist. For the martial artist, the "right environment" is one that evaluates techniques by their effectiveness, not one that favors one art over another. It is also one that is held primarily for the competitor, not the spectator.

The Value of Games

If I stop here you might conclude that Master Funakoshi's fears *have been realized*. I have painted a pretty bleak picture. In light of the importance placed on tournament, trophies, and national ratings, I think the best initial perspective of sport karate is the one you have just seen. However, very little in life is all black or all white, all bad or all good. The same is true of sport karate. There is a good side, a side that benefits the martial artist. To see this, let's examine the subject from two angles. First, let's look at the benefits of free-fighting or sparring (the core of karate competition). After that, we'll look at the benefits of tournament play.

Free-fighting Benefits

There are some schools that discourage free-fighting. They refuse to pursue this form of training because they know that the rules necessary to make it safe must eliminate those really effective techniques (this is the same concern that Funakoshi had about tournaments in the first place). In this sense, they are correct. However, we should not conclude from this that free-fighting is without benefit. Properly used, free-fighting is a valuable training tool. From it, one learns concepts like distance and timing. Applied to self-defense, distance and timing are critical elements that come into play when you have already been hit, knocked down, or are facing an assailant who already has his dukes up. Typical self-defense techniques do not provide everything needed in these situations.

Normally, we avoid those things that will inflame a situation (e.g., you are not standing there in a fighting stance with your guard up at the slightest provocation). But what do you do when you have just been blindsided? Certainly, there is little doubt, then, that you are in a fight. No need to worry about escalating a tense situation into a really ugly one; it's already at that stage.

Self-defense techniques are little help here because they are, by nature, reactive—you react in response to someone else's action. Most self-defense techniques are taught something like this: "You are standing here and someone does this . . ." Or, "You are in this situation when, suddenly . . . !!" But, when it has already come to blows and you have no choice but to fight your way out, how are you going to take the fight to your assailant? What tactics will you use? Suppose your assailant is a trained tournament fighter. Most tournament fighters train hard. They are in shape, and their skills formidable. Not everything is handled from a stationary position with a simple block and counter. How you enter, move, and cover distance in attack and defense become critical in circumstances like these, and it is here that free-fighting is the most beneficial.

But the benefits do not stop there. Sparring also is a great confidence builder. Free-fighting provides the beginning student with a means of self-defense in a relatively short period of time. Normally, competency in any system of self-defense requires years of training. Sparring techniques, on the other hand, are only a small subset of an art's total complement. Being few and relatively simple, sparring techniques require much less time to achieve a minimal level of competence. This superficial level of mastery in a few techniques provides the student with a temporary method of defense until he becomes more proficient in the greater part of the art he studies.

Tournament Play

The competitive element in tournament play adds yet another benefit. Tournament competition gives one the opportunity to face opponents whose techniques and tactics are unfamiliar to him. This forces the student into situations that reveal the spontaneous responses and reactions he is developing (responses he might ultimately use in an actual combat situation). However, here too, we must be careful, for even in the best competitive environment there is the tendency to view noncompetitors as lacking either skill or courage. As one instructor put it, "Tournament fighting . . . promotes and teaches the conquest of others. Competitors often become enamored and inflated with the sense of self that comes from defeating someone else."

This attitude problem is not limited to just the competitors. Too many competitors and spectators alike tend to see tournament fighting as the end—the ultimate demonstration of an individual's martial skill. It may be the ultimate demonstration of skill for those whose arts consist only of sparring techniques tailored for tournaments, but for most martial artists, it doesn't even come close. For the martial artist, viewing fighting competition as anything other than a game and a means to an end is myopic. To believe that tournament play is an accurate reflection of an individual's martial skill is about as accurate as saying all-star professional wrestling is real.

This belief in the validity of tournament play as an indicator of one's real skill is probably the main reason many fighting competitors look down their noses at noncompetitors. Competitors often feel that noncompetitors are afraid to put their skills to the test. They believe that the intensity and stress of fighting competition bring one closer to the reality of actual combat than any other form of training. Granted, competition does raise the adrenaline, intensity, and stress levels for the fighter, but what is it about competition that does this?

Intensity—Real or Imaginary?

For some, the intensity comes from the hope for victory, fame, or momentary glory. For others it is the desire to win the prize (trophy, money, whatever). There also is the stress of performing in front of one's peers, family, and friends. This brings enormous pressure. Finally, there are those for whom the intensity comes simply from fear. However, they shouldn't be looked down on for this, because it is rightly said that "courage is not the absence of fear, but the conquest of it." Fear is both healthy and motivating. Fear keeps us from playing with electricity. It also motivates us to acts of great courage, and fighting competition takes courage. But there is a great difference between fighting in a controlled, safe environment for fame and fortune, and *fighting for your life*.

Fighting in the school or in the tournament ring, for all its benefits, is still only a game of tag (at least that is what it is supposed to be). As such, an individual's participation and subsequent performance in the ring is in no way a true measure of his or her skill or courage.

When it comes to competition, there are those who simply are not motivated to risk a bloody nose, sore ribs, jammed toes, or any other injury for a mere contest. It would be foolish, say, for a dentist—a man who makes his living and supports his family with his hands—to risk injury to those hands in competition. However, I have little doubt that the same individual would willingly risk all, fighting as one possessed, were the safety of his loved ones is at stake. Male grizzly bears are substantially larger than females. As cubs, the males play-fight, but, as adults none of them will take on a female who is protecting her young because she is not play-fighting any more.

There are also some schools that legitimately train for nothing but self-defense, using weapons and tactics that are illegal in sport competition—elbows, knees, leg attacks, ground-fighting, and so on. Jujutsu is a good example. Excluding the handful of schools that claim to train "*only* for combat," just so they can tell everyone else how "bad" they are, competitive events for most self-defense schools, either do not go far enough or are simply impractical. Their non-participation, then, is quite reasonable and no reflection on their student's skill or courage.

To Play or Not To Play

Free-fighting, sparring, and tournament play are neither good nor bad in and of themselves. They are, however, only useful when seen, and used, as one tool among many. Competitors and noncompetitors alike need to remember that a hammer should not be the only tool in one's tool box. (You cannot build a house with just a hammer; neither can you build a house without one.) In this respect, both sides have missed the truth.

Short of life-and-death (or at the very least, save-your-teeth) fighting, there is no way to develop real combat experience or to test one's fighting spirit. As long as tournaments can be found that offer the martial artist a chance to develop and improve his skills, sparring and competitive fighting will continue to be listed as a benefit for self-defense training, because they do come closest to actual combat—in a relatively safe and controlled environment. (At the very least, you face a moving target.)

What sport competitors must avoid is the tendency to view non-competitors as inferior, unskilled, or lacking courage. Noncompetitors, on the other hand, must recognize that sparring and free-fighting (including competitive play) can be useful training tools. They must remember that many tools are necessary for building a house, or developing a well-rounded martial artist. With this mutual understanding and appreciation, both competitors and noncompetitors will come to respect the truth in the other's position, and sport participation will really grow.

◆ ◆ ◆

So, were Master Funakoshi's fears assuaged or realized? The numbers indicate that there definitely has been growth. According to one source, participation in the martial arts has exploded from 9 million Americans a decade ago to 15 million today. If, however, the numbers increase but the quality of martial artists produced from this growth decreases, then the numbers mean nothing.

For myself, I confess that, even after closely examining both sides of this issue, I am less than encouraged at the direction which sport karate seems headed. However, in spite of my misgivings, and despite the many problems inherent in sport karate today, I still believe that we are unwise to dismiss it outright. If nothing else, tournaments do provide the martial artist with a forum for meeting other enthusiasts and exchanging ideas. I continue to make new acquaintances at tournaments and more than a few of them are interesting and capable martial artists. If for no other reason than this, I will continue to support "good" tournaments.

NINE

The Yin Connection: Women and the Martial Arts

I've broken the ribs of a 165-pound male sparring partner, given a nine-inch gash to a World Karate Association champion, and have knocked out several sexist black belts who couldn't believe that a woman could really fight.

—Kathy Long, May, 1992
Black Belt magazine

Throughout this book I have taken the perspective of a self-defense-motivated martial artist. That remains the focus. However, in this chapter, the perspective needs to be refined a bit. Here, I take the only perspective I can: that of a *male martial art instructor*. Although most of what I share here is applicable to both male and female teachers, I believe that female instructors face additional issues that males do not. These issues include the perception that female instructors only teach other women and children and questions about how a female instructor should deal with challenges from her male students. These are issues that I am not qualified to address. My perspective, therefore, can only be that of a male martial art instructor offering instruction to adult men and women.

Historically, women in the East received their martial art instruction privately and from close family members.[1] In America, however, only the smallest minority of students (male or female) are taught privately by family members. American acceptance of feminine equality has thrust women into the modern martial art school. There they train shoulder-to-shoulder with men. But is the female martial art student receiving the training she wants? How do her male training partners feel about working with her? And are there differences or inequities in her training when compared to that of the men?

Realities

Before tackling these questions, we need to come to grips with some basic realities. First, a woman's chances of being attacked by a man are hundreds of times greater than being attacked by another woman. A woman needs, therefore, to train with men. She needs to study with men for the realism

men bring to her self-defense training. Training with a man, a woman gets the feel of her technique as she applies it on the heavier, more muscular masculine body. In this way, she receives a more realistic appreciation of her strengths and abilities.

Men train with men because they, too, will most likely face male assailants. The difference, however, is that a contest between men is physically a much more even match. Even a smaller man has a better chance against a larger man than woman of comparable size has against the same large opponent.

The second reality we must face is that while it is beneficial for women to train with men for self-defense realism, too many men and women choose to ignore the fundamental differences that exist between them. Men ignore them because they do not wish

FIGURE 9–1

to appear chauvinistic. Women ignore them because they believe . . . well, because *some of them* believe they are equal to men in *every* way.

World Champion tournament fighter and kickboxer Bill Wallace caught a lot of flak when, in one of his columns in a popular martial art magazine, he pointed out that, in fighting, women are *not* equal to men (Wallace 1992, 12). Wallace said that women are not physically designed for combat. One reader, in a letter to the editor disparaging Wallace's remarks, said that men are not physically designed for combat either. She is correct, but what Wallace meant was that, relatively speaking, men, being physically stronger than women, are better able to give and take punishment.

Arguments about avoidance and skillful evasion aside, a large part of any fight is still the ability to absorb punishment. Men have much larger bones and approximately 40percent more upper body muscle than women. Paleontologists, for example, can look at a skeleton and immediately identify the individual as male or female simply by bone size and structure. This obvious difference in size means that, in a contest between the two, most women cannot absorb blows to the body as well as a man.

An equally important part of a fight is the ability to inflict punishment. Like it or not, women simply cannot punch as hard as men. Further, their musculature does not afford them the speed advantage necessary to offset the man's natural strength advantage.

In the physical arena, then, we must recognize that women are not equal to men. However, inequality in this area does *not* imply inferiority. Neither does it mean that women are second-class martial artists. They are not. In a street fight, a trained female martial artist can do serious damage to a man (see figures 9–2 through 9–6). Wallace even said as much. In his controversial article, Wallace said that he had no doubt that a female full-contact kickboxing champion "could knock a mugger into tomorrow if he didn't pay attention." However, Wallace also said he believed that in the ring, even a superbly trained female fighter cannot stand up to an equally trained and skilled male opponent in a comparable weight division. This is especially true in the sporting arena, because there the rules actually magnify physical gender differences.

FIGURE 9–2   The assailant may outweigh his intended victim, but this trained martial artist is more than capable of defending herself.

FIGURE 9–3   Deflecting her assailant's unwelcome advance, this defender is about to give someone a free martial art lesson.

FIGURE 9–4   An unexpected, but very effective, left-hand strike to the assailant's groin softens up the defender's larger and stronger opponent.

This truth is a major problem for some—and one they try desperately to deny. To them, "different" means "unequal." "Different," however, is defined as *not alike, dissimilar, not identical, distinct.* This has nothing to do with an individual's merit, worth, skill, position in life, or social standing. Saying that women are different, then, simply acknowledges that, regardless of everything else a woman may be, she is—simply and undeniably—different from a man.

Many examples showing how this physical difference plays out in real-life "battles of the sexes" can be presented. But such arguments are counterproductive, for they only lead us away from meaningful dialogue about differences and how to effectively train with them in mind. For example, I can argue that my 5'10", 175-pound frame is equal to someone 6'3" and 240 pounds. I am wiser, however, focusing on how I can train to better use what I have against my larger and stronger opponent. We must, therefore, move beyond arguments that cloud the issue and onto

FIGURE 9–5   The defender's kick is well placed and quickly incapacitates her hapless assailant.

FIGURE 9–6   Remove the rules that restrict strikes to a handful of targets, and the female martial artist is very capable of defending herself.

relevant matters that actually improve the quality of instruction all students receive—male and female.

Destructive Mind-Sets

The martial arts are open to everyone. Women certainly belong in the arts. If anyone needs self-defense skills, they do. Three out of every four women will face at least one violent crime in their lifetimes. In a day when law-abiding citizens and victims of crime have to wait days or weeks in some states before they can secure arms for personal protection, good self-defense training may be a woman's only option. There remain, however, two contrasting and equally destructive mind-sets that can severely limit a woman's satisfaction and success in the martial arts. They are the "Wimp" and "Feminist" mind-sets.

Wimps

Some women are taught as children that their role is to be helpless, that someone will always take care of them. This is a serious detriment to life in general, but in martial art study, where attitude is everything, it is unthinkable. The reality is that, short of living in a police state, self-protection is ultimately the individual's responsibility. *Wimp thinking* only creates ready-made victims. A classic example of wimp-thinking is the student saying, "Oh, I couldn't do that to anyone," after the instructor demonstrates a particularly aggressive self-defense technique. In a woman or a man, such thinking is self-destructive, and it has no place in the martial arts.

A woman needs to realize that those who will force themselves on her, assaulting and violating her, have no such inhibition. Until she accepts this fact of life, there is little an instructor can do to help the female martial artist achieve her maximum potential.

Feminists

The second self-destructive mind-set is the feminist attitude. Among today's female martial artists, the feminist attitude is actually more common than the wimp. It is also more self-destructive and more difficult to overcome. This mind-set is often characterized by a great deal of hostility toward others (usually toward men, but not always). The individual may not be aware of her hostility, but if it exists, it closes her mind to new ways of thinking.

What makes this feminist attitude particularly dangerous is the false sense of over-confidence it breeds. Some may feel this "overconfidence" is just good-old fighting spirit. But fighting spirit without a strong dose of reality is neither spirit nor courage; it is, rather, foolish bravado.[2]

FIGURE 9–7

FIGURE 9–8

Those blinded by the feminist mind-set must stop viewing all differential treatment as condescending acts of gender inequality. It may not be that at all. For example, in our school we engage in a drill where we blast each other in the abdomen. We wear gloves, but male students drive their blows home with full force. No one, however, strikes the female students with the same vigor. To do so might be considered "equal," but it is also unwise.

All Things Being Equal

In *fighting*, all things being equal, the male practitioner has the advantage. This is the way it is. A female student, then, should not be insulted if her male partner does not attack her with the same aggressiveness that he would another male. Not that a male instructor or training partner should make it easy for her; he should not. But neither should the female training partner attempt to unload on the male student to prove some imagined physical equality.

When sparring with a woman, most men walk a fine line. Aware of their strength and power advantage, they are reluctant to attack a female player with the same intensity as they would another male. No gentleman wants to hurt a lady; neither does he wish to lose to one. (Sensitive big guys have feelings, too, you know.) The dilemma that male martial artists must contend with is, "How do I train with a female partner *without hurting her, without patronizing her, and without looking like I was whipped by her?*" This is a very fine line, indeed.

The problem is compounded when a female partner capitalizes on the male's dilemma and uses the occasion to prove that she can fight like any man. If a man does his best to work with his female partner, he does not deserve to have her attack him with a level of ferocity and intensity that he would

FIGURE 9–9

quickly answer, were the attack coming from another man in the street. If male students are to be considerate of their female partners' feelings regarding condescending attitudes and patronizing conduct, then female students must also consider masculine feelings when they are tempted to go full-bore on a guy who does not deserve it. (Feel free, however, to go all out on the bum who does.)

It is important to remember here that, just as sport karate does not accurately represent the full spectrum of martial arts, neither do wimp- and feminist-thinking female practitioners represent all female martial artists. Clearly, they are a minority. But these two groups receive the lion's share of attention. Like all instructors, I find that 80 percent of my energy is spent on 20 percent of my people. Among female martial artists, those with wimp and feminist attitudes fall squarely into that 20 percent. Pretty unequal, I'd say.

Making the Art Fit the Individual

Training equally means that the instructor does everything possible to make each student's training realistic, challenging, and rewarding. To do this, the instructor tailors the training to match each student's individual abilities to his or her personal needs. Doing otherwise violates the cardinal rule of martial art training: *Make the art fit the individual.* Many instructors routinely make adjustments for their male students. However, the "equality" issue prevents them from doing the same for their female students. This must change! If, in an effort to make the art fit the man, we make adjustments, then we must do the same for a woman.

Equal Contribution

Clearly, male participation contributes significantly to the female student's practice and ultimate success in the martial arts. Women can return the favor. They can begin by making a small investment in protective equipment. Female students (like the males in the class) must wear groin protection. Additionally, they must wear breast protection. These are small but significant steps toward equality in training—and ones that improve everyone's instruction.

The female student's training improves because the realism she needs is provided without the threat of serious injury. Take, for example, learning a defense against a two-hand lapel or chest grab. With breast protection, the male student can grab his female training partner realistically. This is very important.

Most of the time you see the chest grab taught with the grabber using a static, stiff-armed and carefully placed "lapel" grab—hardly realistic. (Muggers and other thugs are not going to be nearly this nice.) Lapel grabs don't always have to be practiced at full force, but they do require some realism. Without it, even if a woman learns a given technique to perfection, her practice will only create a false sense of security.

The male student's training is also improved by his female partner's use of protective equipment. With protective equipment, the male partner has the freedom to attack and strike the same targets on his female partner that he would on another male (again, his most likely assailant). Without protective equipment, his training loses realism.

For example, a technique that requires striking the groin (something done with control even with protective equipment) will be lacking if your partner is not wearing groin protection. You simply cannot simulate a groin strike by hitting the leg or lower abdomen. The fact is that if we train to miss a target, we can be confident that we will miss the target in the street. Neither can you practice a groin strike with perfect (non contact) control. This is because your partner will not react correctly, and the lack of accurate reaction adversely affects your remaining execution and follow-up. Protective equipment solves these problems.[3]

Finally, breast and groin protective equipment reduces any discomfort men might feel from physical contact between the sexes. Gentlemen are often uncomfortable in training situations requiring close physical contact with "unprotected" women. Protective equipment minimizes this because any normally inappropriate or embarrassing physical contact is less disconcerting. (Now, before anyone says that these guys shouldn't feel uncomfortable, consider this: *discomfort* is not a concern to those who are less sensitive and ill-mannered.) Making the female student's male training partner more comfortable, then, will go a long way toward female acceptance in the martial art school.

Equality Training

Equality in martial art training begins with acceptance of this fact: *physically, all are not created equal.* If everyone was the same size and build, and came with the same physical attributes, teaching martial arts would be a lot easier. This is not, however, the case. Still, all students deserve the opportunity to train and study in an environment free of sexual advances, condescending attitudes, and macho behavior. A good teacher (and most teachers are male) can do much to encourage positive participation and discourage negative conduct on the part of his male students. But the responsibility for equality in training rests on more than just masculine shoulders. Female students have an equal responsibility. If female martial artists expect awareness and consideration of their feelings and their training needs from male instructors and training partners—something they have every right to expect—then they, in turn, have a responsibility to acknowledge and consider masculine needs as well.

Acknowledging, accepting, and then training within the constraints of our differences is the only way that real inequality in training will ever disappear. Practical suggestions are just a start, but they are far more realistic than the rhetoric that routinely overshadows this issue. By beginning here, the male and female student alike can train equally, grow, and become the martial artist each is capable of becoming.

TEN

Metaphysical Practice

C*hi, qi,* or *ki* are Chinese and Japanese romanizations of the same Chinese character. *Chi* and *qi* are both pronounced "chee." The difference in spelling results from how they are converted to Roman letters (romanized). Prior to 1979, the Wade-Giles method was used to romanize Chinese words. From that method come such words as *Peking, kung fu,* and *chi.* In 1979 the government of mainland China adopted the Hanyupinyin (or Pinyin) system of romanization. From this method we now have *Beijing, gong fu* and *qi.* In Japanese, *chi* is pronounced, "kee" and is romanized, *ki.*

In a letter to the editor of *Inside Kung-Fu* magazine, W. Bentley Glass (1993, 6) commented,

> Although I have spent 20 years studying various styles of martial arts, both as a class student, and more recently through private instruction from an eighth-degree master, too much still escapes me.
>
> Specifically, as a healthy, disciplined 60-year-old, who is losing raw physical strength thanks to nothing but age, I keep reading and hearing about the so-called development of qi gong (inner strength) and the projection of inner strength. And yet, nowhere do I find how one actually acquires this invisible elusiveness. Not from your magazine, nor from any of my three or four teachers.

Why? [Your magazine] has carried numerous articles alluding to this mystery, all without explanation.

I maintain a very busy schedule. . . . Consequently, I have little time to waste on fiction.

The myths of *chi* power, internal energy, and their application in self-defense abound. Countless articles are published on the subject, and everywhere there are experts making near-miraculous claims about the potential of *chi* and, of course, their ability to use this mysterious and elusive force. This chapter explores this metaphysical aspect of the art, subjecting to close scrutiny *chi*, *chi* power, and those who claim to have mastered it. Returning to reality, it concludes with practical definitions for this "invisible elusiveness" and applications of it that will help us better understand this highly speculative and abstract element of the art.

Some seek instruction in *chi*-power generation because they want an easier way to thwart, repel, or overpower an assailant. We can understand their desire. The healthy and disciplined sixty-year-old martial artist quoted above, for example, is well aware of the limitations that the normal aging process forces on each of us. Cultivating *chi* power to offset this natural erosion seems a reasonable way to go. However, as this gentleman has found, such power is, at best, elusive, and at worst, illusive.

Part of the difficulty in getting our arms around the subject is the paradoxical nature of the word itself. *Chi* is, simultaneously, a very concise and very nebulous term. Its seemingly contradictory linguistic nature means that *chi* is greatly misunderstood. Compounding this is the fact that there are some who, to advance various personal interests, misrepresent this mysterious force.

Writing about *chi*, I am quite frankly tempted to immediately blaze away at those who deliberately lead us astray about *chi* and their ability to control or use it. However, if this study is to fare any better than those that have gone before, then I must resist this temptation and follow a more disciplined and logical course. To that end, the best place to begin is by identifying the primary source or root of *chi* in the martial arts.

Divisible By (At Least) Three

Depending on how fine a line you wish to draw, you can divide Asian martial arts into many different categories. However, for our purposes, only three divisions are necessary:

1. Striking and Grappling
2. Hard and Soft
3. External and Internal.

The difference between striking and grappling arts is obvious: in one, you stand up and fight, while in the other, you fight down in the dirt. Hard and soft are generally referred to as hard-style and soft-style martial arts. The difference between these two is based largely (but not solely) on how much strength and tension are exhibited in the arts' methods of combat. For example, hard styles, like karate and tae kwon do, demonstrate more obvious physical strength and tension (or hardness) in their arts than do the "softer" styles of kung fu. Some kung fu practitioners may rightly dispute this "soft" label, arguing that their arts demonstrate considerable strength. They are correct. Anyone with even a modicum of knowledge in Chinese arts knows that many kung fu systems demonstrate a strength and tenacity that rivals any "hard-style" art. Nevertheless, the hard-style/soft-style division remains widely recognized and understood by most Western martial artists.

But this division crosses more than just striking arts. Grappling arts are similarly divided. Compare, for example, jujutsu and aikido. Although aikido descended from a school of jujutsu it has evolved into a substantially different art. Observe the two, and it quickly becomes apparent that jujutsu

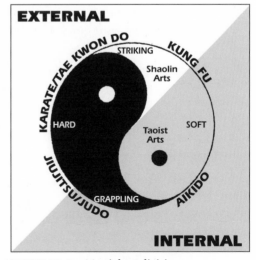

FIGURE 10–1 Martial art divisions.

stands on the hard-style side of the mat, with aikido, landing squarely in the grappling soft-style side. (Judo falls between the two, but much closer to jujutsu than aikido.) A similar comparison might be made between Chinese wrestling (shuai chiao) and China's seizing art, chin-na.

Our last division—*and the one we're most interested in*—knifes across both of the preceding categories—striking and grappling, hard and soft. This division separates *internal* from *external* systems and is represented by the diagonal line running from the top-right corner to the bottom-left corner in figure 10–1.

External and Internal Systems

External systems and fighting arts emphasize strenuous physical training and conditioning as their primary methods for developing effective fighting skills. An externalist, for example, spends many hours conditioning his mind and body and toughening his knuckles, shins, and other personal weapons. For him, the speed and power necessary to overcome potential adversaries comes only from the superbly trained and conditioned body. His maxim is: *Peace through superior firepower.*

Although equally dedicated and vigorous in his training, the internalist spends much less time on toughening his hands and feet, and strenuously conditioning his muscles. Instead, he focuses on technical specifics and *chi* development. For example, an internalist trains continually to develop the optimal stance, precise weight distribution, proper timing, and best lines of force. This means that, among other things, his training regimen includes more slow practice routines than that of the externalist. Bringing all of these elements together perfectly is seen by the internalist as *chi*, or as the result of successful *chi*-power development. Which brings us to the focus of this chapter.

Holy Grail of the Martial Arts

Chi or *ki* is central to the practice of aikido. The name, aikido comes from three words: *ai, ki,* and *do. Ai* means love, harmony, or unification. *Do* means way and, specifically, a spiritual path. (In Chinese, it is the word *tao*.) The second, and central word in all of this is *ki*. *Ki* means breath, awareness, and energy—energy that exists in man and throughout the universe. *Aikido*, then, is the "way of harmony with universal energy." It is said that "the understanding of this original and universal energy plays an essential and primordial part in aikido, in the form of *ki*" and that "Aikido is defined by the way it relates man to the cosmic power, or *ki*" (Random 1992, 206).

Chi is pivotal to China's internal arts as well. Among the Chinese arts, external systems are those whose roots trace back to one of the ancient Shaolin temples. Internal systems, on the other hand, grow from Taoist traditions (note their placement in figure 10–1), and it is here that our problems with *chi* begin.

Taoism (pronounced dao'izm) is a Chinese mystical philosophy. Accepted traditionally as founded by Lao-Tzu sometime between the sixth and fourth centuries BC, Taoism teaches conformity to the *tao* (the way) by unassertive action and simplicity. As a religion, Taoism is often regarded as a corruption of Taoist philosophy. In its evolution from Buddhist-influenced philosophy, the Taoist religion began with the addition of the practice of alchemy: the mixing of elixirs that were intended to ensure immortality. Taoist priest-magicians were acclaimed as spirit mediums and experts in levitation. Among the prominent features of Taoist religion are belief in physical immortality, alchemy, breath control, and a pantheon of deities. As a philosophy-religion, Taoism focuses on obtaining long life and good fortune, frequently by magical means. Magic, then, is the root of *chi* and *chi* power.

Magic

The gamut of possible skills *chi* proponents claim ranges from the ability to do simple physical work; to hurling individuals across a room *without physical contact*; to the development of the use of "Chi Power time control" (Scientific Premium Company, USA 1992, 61)! Having personally witnessed several public and private *chi*-power demonstrations, I must say that I have yet to see one produce effects that can be explained as the result

FIGURE 10–2   My chi protects me.

of *chi* power. In every case, the individual moved, repelled, or affected by *chi* (again, without physical contact) was either one of the *chi* demonstrator's students or simply someone giving in to little more than autosuggestion.

In one impromptu demonstration, a student was blindfolded and placed facing a wall, with his back to the teacher. The teacher, a martial art master with more than a half century in the arts, came up behind the student. Without touching him, he held his hands over the student's shoulders and asked, "Do you feel this?" The student replied, "Yes." The teacher moved his hands to another position and asked the same question. The student, again, replied affirmatively. This was repeated a couple more times with the same result. Finally, the teacher asked, "Where do you feel it?" To which the student pointed blindly behind him in what was obviously the wrong direction. The student then, removed the blindfold and realized how far off he was. The teacher looked at him with an "Oh well" expression on his face, and some of the other students echoed that look suggesting that their fellow had flunked that one, but did he? All the test proved was that the student wanted to feel something, so he felt "something." From my perspective, the student was only gullible; it was the teacher who failed the test.

Autosuggestive effects are hard to prove, and no one wants to embarrass the individuals involved, but *chi* claimants need to be challenged. In no other discipline are practitioners allowed to present purely subjective "feelings" as fact, without offering some way of objectively verifying them. However, in the martial arts, this happens over and over again. Those claiming to possess *chi* get away with making unsubstantiated claims without once having to prove them. Take the case of *chi* "masters" who claim to be able to repel individuals using nothing but *chi*—no tricks, no physical contact —only *chi* energy. (This example is cited because it occurs most

frequently and because of its potential application in self-defense.)

Most of the time, *chi* claimants demonstrate their power on their own students.
When asking for a demonstration with someone *other than one of the claimant's students*—
even offering yourself for the test—you are
usually handed some lame excuse like, "I
would gladly demonstrate my power on you,
but it could very well kill you or at the least,
make you deathly ill, and I cannot assume
that responsibility." When asked to demonstrate on, say, an empty box, you will hear
chi claimants say something like, "Transmitting *chi* on an inanimate object has no effect.

FIGURE 10–3

It only works on living things." (I beg your pardon. I thought *chi* existed
in everything.) Ask them to affect, then, a living (potted) plant—make it
wilt or something—and you receive another lame and condescending
excuse like, "How can you expect me to use my power to harm this poor
plant?" (I'll bet that I can use my *chi* power to make that plant lean toward
a sunlit window!)☺

If these *chi* practitioners actually possess this illusive force, they seem
not to have mastered it, for they are unable to control it beyond either full
"on" and "off" (except, again, with their own students). This is like the
used car salesman saying, "This Ferrari is capable of zero or 200 miles per
hour, but not 15, 30, or anything in between." The exotic *chi* racer, it seems,
can run you down, but it cannot be parked! Curiously, most of us can control our external, inanimate, several-thousand-pound motor vehicles with
greater precision than *chi* masters can control their own *internal* power. *Chi*
may be an elusive force, but based on some of the excuses given for not
submitting it to verifiable tests, it is downright slippery.

I admit that all of the *chi* charlatans have left me more than a little
skeptical, but I am not the only one. One respected t'ai chi player with

more than a score of years in the art (t'ai chi, like aikido, is an art that directs and utilizes *chi* in its training and application), hit the nail on the head when he said,

> During most of my tenure as a martial artist, qi has been represented to me as a 'Life Force' which, in a magnificent nose-thumbing way, was immeasurable to that poor sap, the Western scientist (Sigman 1992, 6).

In describing the exercises that develop this "Life Force," he went on to say that,

> Whatever "qi" was, qigongs were ritualistic exercises which were reputed to develop it. In other words, qigongs developed the unexplainable in unexplained ways.

Electromagnetic Force?

The smoke and mirror, magical descriptions *chi* claimants foist on us sound strangely similar to early scientific descriptions of electricity. For the longest time, an accurate definition of electricity eluded us. Even today, a definition that the layman can fathom is beyond most of us. However, as unexplainable as electricity was, we at least understood its laws. We knew, for example, how to generate it, how to store it, and how to put it to useful work. We knew very well (and in some very concrete, explainable, and reproducible ways) how to use electricity. Even a child could control its flow and harness its power with just one tiny finger. And all of this was possible before we could accurately explain exactly what it was.

The same is true for magnetism. Long before men knew exactly what it was, they knew how to use it. Moreover, the needle pointing north worked for everyone who tried it.

Chi's parallel with electricity and electromagnetic force is not new. More than a few have described *chi* as along these lines. The major difference, however, is that the effects and properties of electricity and electromagnetic force are known, reproducible, and verifiable. The effects and properties of *chi*—so far anyway—are *not*.

The physical capabilities and theories of Asian fighting arts have been tested repeatedly and proven to work. Noncontact *chi* power, on the other hand, has not. It is magic; nothing more. But rejecting noncontact *chi* as magic still leaves us with a problem. How do we explain the almost supernatural feats performed by some highly credible martial art masters—feats that appear well beyond the individual's physical capabilities? I'm not talking about the ability to break flaming boards, tall stacks of bricks, or slabs of ice—those are merely side show tricks designed to attract customers. What I am talking about are the incredible skills and abilities legitimate masters of the art often possess.

FIGURE 10–4   Morihei Ueshiba, 1883–1969.

The Real Thing?

Aikido founder Morihei Ueshiba routinely demonstrated his ability to throw students around with what looked like barely a touch, and his ability to do this continued well into old age. Excusing those students who let themselves be thrown, and discounting the fact that in aikido you are taught not only how to fall, but how to fall beautifully, and we are still left with the reality that Ueshiba's near-miraculous feats have some basis in fact. Regardless of how inflated the man's now legendary abilities loom today, the fact remains that by all accounts Ueshiba really did send attackers flying. The question for us is, how?

Chi Descriptions— From Allegorical To Literal

Apart from the outlandish claims of *chi* charlatans, I think that the problem is not one of whether or not individuals use *chi*, but one of correctly understanding what the *chi* they use really is. Consider the following Eastern description of a blow as it is delivered with *chi*: *Pulling or borrowing chi from the earth, you channel this energy through your foot and leg, to the tan tien* [the body's *chi* center], *finally releasing it through your arm and to your opponent.*

Describing the same action in Western terms, and you get something like this: *Starting from a solid base and beginning with the foot, the calf and thigh muscles contract. The hip then, rotates and sinks into the movement adding mass to the acceleration of the arm as it is thrust forward, striking the target.*

The Eastern description of the punching process—"borrowing *chi* from the earth"—is allegorical. It represents a physical process in abstract, almost spiritual, terms. The Western description, on the other hand, is (to our thinking) literal. For us, the same punching process is simply the neuromuscular sequence of material events necessary to deliver a single punch or blow with staggering, almost unbelievable power. However, the phrases "physical process" and "material events," although accurate, lead us to the narrowest conception of what *chi* really is. Even devoid of its magical connotations, *chi* is still more than a purely physical process or event.

Synergy

Perhaps the best Western word for capturing the essence of chi is synergy. Synergy is a combined action or operation. A synergistic cooperative effort is one whose total effect is greater than the sum of the effects taken independently. Look at it like this. Let's assign an arbitrary value of two to each of the following:

strength = 2
speed   = 2
timing   = 2
breath   = 2
intensity = 2

Taken together, the five elements listed add up to ten. However, applied cooperatively, that is, synergistically, their collective effort may be many times greater than the sum of the individual elements.[1] This is what Ed

Parker meant when he described chi as follows in his Infinite Insights into Kenpo, Volume One (1982, vii).

> ... the state of the body and mind where one obtains the maximum force of his body. It involves total and complete synchronization of mind, breath, and strength to achieve maximum focus. It is that extra inner force created by the precise synchronization of mind, breath, and strength.

"Synchronization" is the operative word here. I believe that synchronization is what Miyamoto Musashi, the most famous of Japan's swordsmen, referred to when he said that "There is timing in everything. Timing in strategy cannot be mastered without a great deal of practice." Synergy or *Chi* cannot happen without timing, and timing is—as Parker put it, "complete synchronization of mind, breath, and strength."

Combining Parker's definition with Musashi's remarks about timing and the practice necessary to develop it, and *chi* becomes something that flows from the mental imprint of a well-practiced technique or movement. When required, the mind follows this imprint instinctively, flowing with singleness of purpose, calmness of mind, and a complete coordination between mental and physical that is practically unstoppable. This *chi*, this *synergy*, then, is a precise moment in time when the mind, will, and emotions are in complete and total harmony with an adrenaline-charged body. In that instant, the fighter, by virtue of bringing all of the mental and physical elements together perfectly, performs at a level that extends well beyond his observable physical abilities.

Thus far, in our effort to understand *chi* we have examined its Taoist origins, removed its magic, found a comparable and equally concise Western word for its practical aspect, and compiled a logical definition of this "invisible elusiveness." But to see how *chi* manifests itself in actual application we need to change our perspective from the practitioner and his training, to one that focuses on the effects. What happens when this synergy or *chi* comes together in a self-defense technique?. Let's take two movements (remember, movements are parts of techniques) and see how external application might differ from an internal one. We'll begin with an externalist's defense against a right punch.

External and Internal Application

After blocking his assailant's punch with a right arm, the skilled externalist executes a right flat-fist strike to the left side of his opponent's face as in figures 10–5 and 10–6. (This is a real head-rattling, jaw-breaking defense.) From the force of the blow, the attacker may be knocked down; he may even be rendered unconscious. In any event, the movement is very effective and the damage—a broken jaw—is substantial.

A similar defense by an internalist also begins with a right arm redirecting the assailant's blow (figure 10–7). Instead of the flat-fist, though, the internalist's counterattack is a right palm strike to the left side of the attacker's face (figure 10–8). This may look like an inferior blow, but it is not, for the right palm is only half of the movement. Simultaneous with the right palm strike, the internalist's left hand slaps the back of his assailant's right shoulder. This effectively (and painfully) twists the attacker's neck by rotating his head clockwise (with the right hand) while, simultaneously, thrusting his shoulder in the opposite direction (with the left hand).

This defensive movement is clearly not as head-rattling as the preceding one. The assailant's jaw is neither distended nor swollen. However,

FIGURE 10–5   Blocking opponent's right punch.

FIGURE 10–6   Right flat-fist strike.

FIGURE 10–7   Redirecting opponent's right punch.

FIGURE 10–8   Shearing palm (opposing forces).

his incapacitation is just as immediate and just as effective. Instead of a broken jaw, the opponent suffers severe neck trauma. By timing his right palm to the face with the simultaneous left palm strike to the back of the attacker's shoulder, the defender forces the assailant's head to rotate well past its normal limit, resulting in cervical disc, vertebrae, or ligament damage. (Having had neck surgery myself, I can personally vouch for just how painful and disabling a neck injury can be.)

Although incapable of probing the depths of difference that exist between internal and external fighting methods, these two *very* simple examples clearly show that internal techniques require a significantly higher level of sophistication than do similar techniques from most external systems. This is because more elements must come together at precisely the right instant to produce their disabling effect (again, synergy). The effectiveness of *bringing together* many elements is obvious when comparing two tried-and-true weapons, the war club and the modern semiautomatic handgun.

Both the war club and the modern handgun have proven themselves in combat. When it comes to self-defense, a baseball bat (the modern equivalent of a war club) is a very potent weapon. It has no moving parts to malfunction, and it requires minimal skill to wield effectively—two very strong points in its favor. On the other hand, the .45-caliber semiautomatic handgun has many moving parts, any number of which are much more vulnerable to damage than the ball bat. Moreover, considerably greater skill is necessary to master the handgun. Compared to the bat, then, these differences would seem to make the handgun less desirable than the bat. Still, in a life-threatening situation, I think it is fair to say that most of us would much rather have the handgun.

Lest we think that one system is necessarily better than the other, remember that both methods, although fundamentally different, are still very effective. External arts are, I believe, better suited to younger practitioners. Conversely, internal systems are more beneficial for practitioners with decades of training under their belts. I say this because "mature" practitioners—by virtue of their many years of practice—possess the higher skill level and precision necessary to make internal techniques work. That said, let me quickly add that we benefit most when we recognize the value in both systems.

Consider what happens when the defender combines the externalist's right flat-fist that you saw in figure 10–6, with the internalist's shearing palm strike to the back of his assailant's right shoulder (figure 10–8). Figure 10–9 shows this *external-internal* application. Here, the attacker suffers not only a painfully broken jaw, but severe neck trauma as well. A handful of highly effective hybrid fighting systems have evolved through such combinations of internal and external training and fighting methods. Known as internal-external or external-internal systems (the first word indicating the primary emphasis) these systems actually represent the *creme de la creme* of fighting arts.

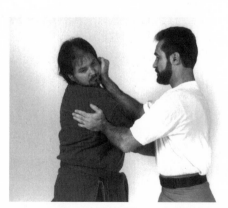

FIGURE 10–9 · Right flat-fist with shearing palm.

Some Key Points

The human mind is capable of incredible things. Its potential is not even remotely understood, much less used. Doubtless, the body possesses and generates energy. Thermographs show that we radiate heat energy. Electroencephalographs record electrical activity in the brain. These are two known and verifiable energies we possess. Two hundred years ago these things were unknown, and the prevalent theories of that day have, for the most part, been completely disproved or replaced by others. Who then, is to say that 200 years from now, our theories will not suffer the same fate? From that perspective, I leave myself cautiously open to the possibility of another, still unknown, energy source within. I say "cautiously open," because whatever energy source or inner power is discovered, it must be verifiable, reproducible, and stand up to close scientific scrutiny. Until then, I see nothing but danger in the unquestioned acceptance of some mystical power in martial art practice.

The Danger in Chi

The belief in a mystical, magical, or metaphysical *chi* is potentially destructive to the martial artist. If, for example, you believe that your opponent has such a power, it may lead to irrational behavior (much like the Chinese Boxers belief of invincibility—they seriously overestimated their internal power and underestimated the power of Western bullets). In a practical sense, you might not attack when you should, or you might attack when you should not. You might neglect necessary physical conditioning and training, believing that you are in full possession of a more powerful force. In a confrontation, you might expect your magical *chi* to stop your

FIGURE 10–10   His chi protected him alright.

137

attacker, only to find your own "force field" painfully and embarrassingly penetrated by a big fist in your face.

As a viable part of the martial artist's arsenal, *chi*, and specifically non-contact *chi*, is dubious, at best—at least as long as its proponents continue to babble definitions that defy understanding and claim examples of its power that remain clearly in the unproven realm of folklore. Until proof is presented—not "more" proof, for we have none, as yet—we will have to settle for a *chi* that is *a synergistic, near-perfect union of mind, body, and spirit for the accomplishment of a specific task*—which in our case is effective self-defense. This kind of logical definition removes the shroud of mystery from the elusive *chi* and strips it of its undeserved "metaphysical" label.

Ed Parker (1982, 3) summed it up beautifully when he said, "It must be remembered that whenever a subject develops definable qualities, when the unknown becomes known, the mysticism disappears. Martial arts are a real and tangible subject." A real and tangible definition of *chi* actually facilitates sound martial art study, for it makes the student work as much on perfecting his technique as he does on his physical conditioning. The axiom "perfect technique comes from perfect practice" is as true today as it ever was. *Chi* or no, there is still no shortcut to real martial skill.

ELEVEN

The Spiritual Dimension

The Zen master brings his pupil to enlightenment, not by expo-
sition, explanation, or example. Rather, it is carried out by posing a puzzle (known as a koan), by silence in response to a question, or by a slap in response to an answer.

—Steve Liszewski, 1995
(paraphrased)
The Client/Server Observer

In addressing the value of tradition in Chapter 5, I pointed out that Eastern martial art evolution was far ahead of its Western counterpart, not
only in the physical realm, but also in its intellectual, moral, and spiritual development. I use the past tense verb "was" because I believe that
in many areas American martial artists and their arts have grown and developed beyond their classical roots. However, in that chapter I address only
the intellectual and moral issues. In the last chapter, Chapter 10, you saw
an example of how Eastern religion and thought influence the arts. The
example there was the way that *Taoist* beliefs in magic led to the erroneous
teaching of *chi* power generation. But Eastern religion also influences the
art in other, less theatrical ways. Beginning with arguments favoring formal Eastern religious and spiritual instruction as part of martial art training,

this chapter examines this spiritual dimension of the art and assesses its need, desirability, and relevance in contemporary American society.

Spiritual Training as Part of Martial Art Study

There are, within the martial art community, those who contend that omission of the religious, spiritual, and meditative elements from martial art instruction limits the practitioner's training and development: both as a martial artist and as a contributing member of society. They note that in many culturally Western martial art schools today, very few value the role of formal Eastern meditation, either as a method of self-discovery or as a means of enlightenment.

In an article in a scholarly martial art magazine, Michael Maliszewski (1992, 1:36), for example, disparages the fact that many consummate Western martial artists—highly skilled and accomplished individuals—immerse themselves in the physical side of their respective arts, all the while perfectly content to ignore (and in some cases, deliberately exclude) the art's religious and spiritual elements. Martial art publications, he notes, are replete with stories of individuals who are attracted to the arts solely for self-defense. In this, he is correct. However, it is also his contention that those pursuing martial art study for this reason alone suffer from feelings of inadequacy, physical impotence, and inferiority. He acknowledges that the meditative, religious, and spiritual elements are *not* necessary to produce technically proficient practitioners; however, he contends that individuals so trained remain psychologically immature and incapable of dealing with conflict in non-violent ways.

His argument is not new—extreme, but not new. Others before him have likewise complained that the wrongs in American martial arts today are directly attributable to this lack of a contemplative and meditative component in martial art training. But are our shortcomings "directly attributable" to this omission? Is there any evidence supporting the contention that inclusion of spiritual instruction produces better, more socially responsible martial artists?

Without a doubt, American martial arts have their share of problems, but so do their Asian counterparts. For all of the ethereal instruction Asian practitioners supposedly receive, they, too, are plagued with their share of unscrupulous instructors, unruly practitioners, splits and divisive factions in their organizations, power politics among their leaders, and a jingoistic attitude toward non-Asian students that rivals anything in the United States. If *Eastern* meditation, as a method of self-discovery and a means of enlightenment, works no better than this in its own culture, then I have little hope for its effectiveness in our very different Western culture.

Avoiding Religious and Spiritual Elements

Recall for a moment the opening quotation from Geoff Gleeson in the Introduction.

> When a skill or sport is transferred to another country, that country should replace the foreign training methods with methods reflecting and exploiting its own characteristics, needs, and virtues.

Gleeson's Rule, as I call it, is the central truth running through this book. The preceding chapters make a strong case for adopting this rule in our physical training. Practical application of the same rule in the spiritual dimension means that those training in Saudi Arabia, for example, draw from that nation's Muslim heritage and faith. Formal spiritual instruction and meditative practice there should conform to Islam's culture and customs. In Israel, practitioners would incorporate training methods compatible with Jewish practices and tradition. Likewise, in the United States, we replace incompatible foreign training methods with those that reflect our own "community" characteristics, needs, and virtues. In America, however, this is much more difficult than it sounds.

Most Heterogeneous Nation

Many are probably familiar with the acronym MFN. It stands for *Most Favored Nation*. As a provision of a trade agreement, MFN extends to another nation certain automatic rights and trade advantages in its commerce with the United States—advantages that countries without MFN do not have. MHN, or *Most Heterogeneous Nation*, is a designation that—if it actually existed—would apply exclusively to the United States. This is because America is, unquestionably, the most ethnically and culturally heterogeneous nation on earth. With possibly one exception, no other country even comes close.

Our closest competitor for the MHN designation is, perhaps, Indonesia. The fifth most populous nation in the world, Indonesia has more than 300 distinct people groups. Culturally, Indonesia is the most diverse of the nations of the East. Certainly she is much more diverse than the very homogenous nations of China, Japan, and Korea—nations from which most of America's more popular martial arts have come.

Partly because of past European colonial ambitions, and partly because military and economic alliances there foster greater cultural movement and integration, Europe today, has a more heterogeneous population than many nations of the East—certainly the Far East. Many European countries, for example, have sizable emigrant communities. France has very large African and Asian populations, and Germany has one of the largest Turkish communities outside Turkey. The Netherlands, Great Britain, and other European nations can all make similar claims. Still, when it comes to multicultural diversity, all of these pale in comparison to America's immigration legacy.

I point this out not to say that American culture is better or worse than any other, but only to say that ours is very different and substantially more diverse than any in the East. Given this ethnic diversity and multicultural perspective, I believe that there are some very compelling reasons why American martial artists pursue physical excellence in their arts—*to the exclusion of Eastern spiritual, religious, and meditative elements.*

American cultural diversity affords its citizens unparalleled access to more than just different fighting arts. We also have a wealth of world religions and philosophies that we are guaranteed, by our constitution, the freedom to examine and explore. We may, for example, freely pursue Hinduism, Buddhism, Islam, Judaism, Christianity, atheism, humanism, naturalism, and every other '-ism' in between. All of this apart from the art.

Americans have an abundance of social, cultural, intellectual, philosophical, spiritual and religious avenues available to them: self-help programs, college courses in ethnic studies, and religious and spiritual instruction, just to name a few. With all of this available to him, the American martial artist may avoid the religious and spiritual elements inherent in Eastern martial arts simply because he already feels that his spiritual needs are adequately addressed through any one of these other venues.

Equally important in a pluralistic and multicultural society is the recognition that what is acceptable for some is culturally taboo for others. For example, the martial art practitioner may distance himself from the art's spiritual and religious components because they are—from his culture's perspective—forbidden. The practicing Muslim, orthodox Jew, or evangelical Christian may rightly pursue martial art study and training for self-defense, health, or sport reasons; however, his religious laws and beliefs are generally incompatible with Eastern religious teaching.[1] Because of this incompatibility, many practitioners of Western faiths (and for that matter, members of any number of other religions) are prohibited from participating in the religious or spiritual aspects of Eastern martial arts.

Focus on Physical Excellence

On the practical side, there are practitioners who focus exclusively on the physical elements of the art simply because of the time constraints forced on them by everyday life. If life's demands compel you to focus strictly on the physical aspects of the art to the exclusion of the spiritual dimension, is it fair to say that you suffer from feelings of inadequacy, physical impotence, or inferiority? As a microcosm of society, the martial arts, I am sure, have their share of participants who feel inadequate, physically impotent, and inferior; however, the same can be said about any number of those who follow any pursuit. For example, an attorney's quest for excellence and mastery of the law can be interpreted as his way of dealing with similar feelings. What better way to satisfy one's need for self-protection and

FIGURE 11–1   Can we say that feelings of inadequacy, physical impotence, or inferiority motivate individuals to study and master the law?

gain some measure of personal control in our highly litigious society than to master the law? The same argument can be made for any number of persons and their professions, from clerics, to police officers, to Ph.D's, to politicians.

And what of the practitioner who suffers from feelings of inadequacy, physical impotence, and inferiority? Cannot the *physical* practice of martial arts actually be therapeutic? More often than not, the confidence we gain from physical martial art training shows up in the form of less violence in our lives, not more. It is the truly impotent individual who, lacking such confidence, angrily storms out of the office, only to return later with a gun. Not so the one who, through years of exercising self-discipline, trains and studies day in and day out, perfecting his formidable physical skills. Overcoming the many challenges associated with hard physical training teaches the practitioner to master and control both the violence within and the fears that feed it.

The contention that *martial art study and practice devoid of the religious, spiritual, and meditative elements* leaves practitioners "psychologically immature and incapable of dealing with conflict in nonviolent ways" is wrong. It is wrong because it fails to consider the untold numbers of practitioners who, by virtue of their efforts and subsequent accomplishments through physical training, are *very mature and more than capable of dealing with conflict in nonviolent ways.* Although there are many other reasons why martial art instructors avoid this spiritual side of the art, I will share only one more: adjunctive training.

Adjunctive Instruction?

An *adjunct* is something added to something else. The adjunct is not essentially part of the thing it is added to. Eastern religious, spiritual, and med-

itative elements are adjuncts. They have been added to martial art training. They are not an essential part of the art. Lest these statements mislead
you, please understand that my opposition to formal Eastern spiritual
instruction as a part of martial art training and study is not because I disagree with the need; on the contrary, I believe the need for a strong positive spiritual influence in our society as a whole is greater today than ever.
No, I oppose incorporation of the spiritual element precisely because I
believe that this area of life is so important that it deserves more than just
adjunctive treatment.

In Chapter 5, I addressed the issue of learning a foreign language as
part of martial art instruction—for instance, learning Japanese in a karate
school. Despite a student's best efforts at learning and pronouncing such
things as *kiba-dachi, mae-geri,* and *seiken chudan uchiuke gedan-barai,*[2] he
still would not know enough Japanese to locate even a lavatory. Under the
constant tutelage of qualified language teachers and eight-hour-a-day
lessons, it takes months of formal instruction, followed by decades of practice, to master another language. Given these realities, can we really expect
to achieve spiritual enlightenment through even the best adjunctive lip
service?

Martial Art Spiritual Training— Adding Value?

Recognizing that lasting spiritual enlightenment is simply not possible
when approached in such a superficial manner, we are still left with the
question, "Is there *any* value to formal spiritual instruction in modern martial art training?" I think the answer is yes and no. For those pursuing the
art for reasons other than self-defense, probably, yes. But what of those
students who are paying their hard-earned money for *martial art* instruction?

Even eliminating those instructors who spend time teaching the spiritual side of the art simply to cover their lack of knowledge or skill in the
physical area, we are still left with the fact that every minute spent on spiritual development is one less moment spent in practical physical instruc-

tion. If, for example, I enroll in a firearms class for self-protection, I expect to learn something of the legal limitations, ramifications, and ethical consequences of defending life and property with deadly force. I expect this. I do not, however, expect to receive instruction in self-discovery and enlightenment. Neither do martial artists.

Where does all of this leave the Western student? How does he handle routine school or dojo practices that have religious connotations? Well, in Chapter 5, I addressed one of them: bowing. There, I pointed out how bowing before a school shrine or alter may be seen by some as a sign of reverence or religious obeisance to another spiritual leader or guide. To American students of Muslim and Jewish faiths, this practice is not simply acquainting yourself with another culture's traditions; it is nothing short of partaking in a forbidden religious practice. Since it was covered before, I will not rehash the issue further. However, another much more common Eastern religious practice is meditation.

Meditation and Visualization

Meditation is taught in all of the world's great religions—Eastern and Western. Because of this, its religious significance is quickly recognized by many. Separated from any spiritual connotation, meditation by itself is a useful training tool. Where meditation becomes a thorny issue is in the *purpose* of the practice. As a guest instructor in another school, I remember privately being asked by a student about his school's practice of meditation. In his school, everyone meditated for the last five to ten minutes of class. To him, as a devout Catholic, the idea of meditating for the purpose of emptying his mind, centering himself, realizing his essential nature, or seeking enlightenment, rang of Eastern religion and New Age thinking. Although he enjoyed the physical training he was receiving, he was more than a little uncomfortable with this one practice. As you can see, martial art instructors need to be careful when using meditation as a method of training. At the very least they owe their students a straightforward explanation of its purpose within the school. Then the individual student can decide whether or not he or she wishes to participate. (My advice to the student, by the way, was this: since his instructor did not require him to meditate on this or that, then he was free meditate on whatever he wished. He could meditate on spiritual things compatible with his faith, the physical skills he was just learning, or anything else he felt was beneficial.)

Meditation in some schools is really little more than visualization. Visualization, because of its use by New Age groups, has really received an undeserved bad reputation. However, using imagination to train physical skills violates none of the principles or teachings of the Koran or Jewish and Christian religious texts. It is, therefore, completely acceptable to teach meditation as a tool to perfect technique, to rehearse and mentally practice, and to focus your mind and atten-

FIGURE 11–2   Practical visualization.

tion in a positive, productive, and practical way. Presented in this manner—without the weight of spiritual or religious significance—meditation is a useful and *acceptable* training tool.

I emphasize the word "acceptable" here because, as a very busy martial artist and martial art teacher with equally overworked students, I struggle with anything that infringes on precious training time—my student's or my own. When it comes to meditation and visualization, you can, for example, mentally rehearse your practice and review the things that you were working in class while commuting to and from work. This you do by yourself. Class time, on the other hand, provides some things you do not have readily available most of the time: qualified instructors, training equipment, and training partners. Unless meditating *en masse* (as a class for the purpose of visualization or anything else) imparts some "special" training benefit, I think that its practice as part of martial art training, is one that is best left to the student's own initiative.

Morality and Spiritual Need

Throughout this book the perspective has been that of the dedicated martial artist. Early on, I defined this individual as one whose primary interest in and motivation for study is excellence in self-defense. I have gone to great lengths to make it clear that mastery in this one area does not exclude investigation, study, assimilation, and even integration of the other areas of interest offered by the many martial arts. In fact, I firmly believe that excellence in self-defense must extend beyond just the physical arena.

High intellectual and moral standards are required of teacher and student alike. Spiritual awareness and the need to realize one's essential nature by attaining optimal intellectual and spiritual development are much more important than any physical skill we may ever develop. Where, then, is the balance? How do conscientious teachers of martial arts pass on their formidable physical skills in a responsible way, without imposing their personal beliefs on those who may not want them? How do we share our spiritual beliefs with those who do wish to hear them without stepping on the toes of others? Like many instructors, I believe we do this first by example.

As teachers, we exercise a degree of authority and influence over those who choose to train and study with us. However, the fact remains that our students will follow our *examples* farther than they will ever follow our *words*. Wielding influence effectively means demonstrating our personal spiritual and religious convictions in our everyday lives. If, in that effort, my students notice something different in me, and question it, then I tell them frankly and openly what it is. If they wish to know more, then I make time—outside our martial training—to share with them the source of my conviction, strength, and inner peace. This presents, I believe, a fuller, life-size portrait of exactly how the dedicated martial artist lives and functions as a contributing member of society.

Replacing Form with Function

As humans we are simultaneously physical, intellectual, and spiritual beings. As such, we need exercise to keep us both physically and mentally fit. We need intellectual stimulation and challenge to stay sharp and improve our powers of perception and reason. Most important, we need awareness of the infinitely greater forces that exist around us.

Given the importance of the spiritual dimension, its deeply personal nature, and the complexities of sharing one's religious beliefs in our multicultural, pluralistic, and highly diverse social environment, perhaps the best application of Gleeson's Rule is one that replaces form with function. Instead of bringing formal meditation and other Eastern religious trappings into Western martial art study and training, try sharing your religious or spiritual beliefs by personal example. Honestly living them before your pupils will have a much greater impact on their lives than any amount of formal instruction.

◆ ◆ ◆

A special thanks to Mr. Kurt Frankenburg, a teacher of martial arts whose enthusiasm encourages us and whose wisdom far exceeds his years.

TWELVE

Yellow Pages Master

C learly, unquestioned adherence to Eastern training methods and practices poses many problems for the Western martial art student. In fairness, though, not all of the problems spring from our arts' Asian roots. For example, in discussing the value of tradition in Chapter Five, I pointed out how, in the absence of positive character-building traditions, culturally Western martial arts developed some very negative character traits of their own. Also, it should be clear from the discussion of sport karate in Chapter 8, that Western individualism in general and American competitiveness in particular are the major reasons why American sport fighters look down on those who do not likewise enter the arena. Before concluding this book, allow me to take a more light-hearted approach to another decidedly American martial art problem: namely—commercialism, and its impact on the coveted black belt.

FIGURE 12–1

In the four years from 1992 through 1995, Yellow Pages martial art listings in our area have jumped from 98 to 136. This 39 percent increase means that competition for students is stiff. In an effort to increase market share, many instructors resort to what has become an annual event in one-upmanship. The spectacle begins early in November and occurs concurrently in communities across the country. If past performances are any indicator, then this year's show promises to be as sensational as ever. Yes, sports fans, coming soon to homes everywhere: the annual Yellow Pages promotions.

Leafing through the recent telephone record and searching the nearly 140 *different* martial art schools and organizations currently listed in our area, I found no less than one tenth-degree black belt, two ninth-degrees, four eighths, five sevenths, two sixths, and two fifths. (About the only thing missing was "... and a partridge in a pear tree.") There are also numerous Masters, Grandmasters, Grand Masters (they're really grand), and the occasional Professor. With so many masters and grandmasters around, some now opt for combination titles like Chief Grand Master, Master-Teacher, and Master Shihan. (If *shihan* means "master teacher," does *master shihan* mean "master-master teacher?") Further dividing the master category are American Masters, Certified Masters, and one apparently ultimate, *The* Master. (Combining these titles is amusing, if not accurate: "*THE* Certifiable American Master.") All of these with the usual assortment of World Famous and World Champions (small world, huh?). I'll bet you didn't know that our community was so rich in martial talent, now did you?.

But, there was one blight on those bright yellow pages. Amongst all of these highly credentialed luminaries was one advertisement that had the bare-faced, unmitigated gall to boldly proclaim its chief instructor's rank as a ... *third degree black belt*! "Unbelievable," some might say. "This guy says he has trained for nearly thirty years, and yet he is still only a third degree black belt? The guy down the street [just about any street] has been in the martial arts for just ten years, and he is already several degrees above this fellow. What gives?"

In fairness, some of the titles listed in the Yellow Pages are legitimate. For example, in some Korean arts, those holding sixth degree black belts and higher are permitted to use the title of "master." Those with an eighth dan and higher may use the title "grandmaster." It must be pointed out that, as one writer noted, grandmaster (as used here) means, for example, a grandmaster *in* tae kwon do, and not the grandmaster *of* tae kwon do. That aside, there are still too many self-promotions in the arts (only the self-promoted need write to complain).

Anyway, being an area resident since 1964, I have had ample opportunity to follow these annual promotions, and I find it amazing how fast some of these individuals move up in rank. Oh, I'm sure that everyone listed in the phone book can produce a certificate backing up their claimed rank, but too many certificates are, like many of today's black belts, less than what they imply.

How Much is that Black Belt in the Window?

There are many reasons for this situation, but the upshot of it is a cheapening of the coveted black belt. A black belt, today, simply doesn't mean what it used to. It used to be that even a first degree black belt certificate represented somewhere between seven and ten years of hard work. Now, some schools advertise that you can receive a black belt in two or three years; eighteen months by mail-order. Walk into many commercial martial art schools today and you are pressured to sign up for the "Black Belt" program. Pay X-number-of-dollars (make that XXXX-dollars), and in less time than it takes to earn a college degree, you can have your very own black belt.

I am not faulting anyone for wanting to make a decent living teaching martial arts.

FIGURE 12–2 "In no time at all you'll have your very own black belt."

FIGURE 12–3   "Yup, it's time for another stripe."

I am, however, faulting those who flatly and flagrantly "sell" belts. No wonder so many martial artists—even experienced martial artists—now claim ridiculously high ranks and bloated titles. After giving away or selling black belts to every Tom, Dick, and Harry, about the only way instructors can distinguish themselves from their students is to claim rank that is beyond their own progeny.

Where will it end? Supreme Grandmaster? Ultimate Grandmaster? Great Supreme Ultimate Grandmaster? Sadly, even the late kenpo master William Chow fell prey to this ugly monster. In the second edition of *Who's Who in American Martial Arts,* published in 1985, Chow's rank is listed as fifteenth degree black belt. If anyone deserved recognition for his skill in the martial arts, he certainly did; but his titles of Professor, Grandmaster, and fifteenth degree black belt came about precisely because belts had become so cheap that even his credentials had to be pumped up to be recognized.

The pressure to make everyone equal in our society has also contributed to the erosion of the coveted black belt. Today we are told that everyone can be a black belt— regardless of age or physical ability. The truth is, however, that not everyone can become a black belt—not in the original sense of the rank. There are a variety of mental and physical conditions that prohibit many from reaching expert level, and in case anyone forgot, black belt is supposed to mean expert.[1] For example, karate is defined as "an Oriental art of self-defense in which an attacker is disabled by crippling kicks and punches."

In reality, an 8-year-old black belt is incapable of delivering such blows. Moreover, the requirement to kick effectively is a barrier to one confined to a wheelchair. Proficiency in other areas of the art may well be within reach of one so impaired, but black belt level is very likely not.[2]

I am not saying that a black belt is based solely on physical skill; it is not. Black belt rank stands for much, much more than just the ability to kick and punch. A black belt, even a first degree black belt, must possess more than technical proficiency. He must also possess a maturity greatly exceeding his skill (boy, that disqualifies a lot of us on the spot). A black belt must also have an understanding of the principles employed in his art and be able to pass that knowledge, skill, leadership, and maturity on to others in a precise, clear, and systematic manner. All of these things are what make a "black belt," a *black belt*.

Excess Baggage

But, back for a moment to our highly credentialed luminaries. You really have to feel sorry for them. Think of it: they have so much excess baggage to carry around. How can they, for example, possibly learn from anyone? After all, hasn't a ninth or tenth degree grandmaster just about learned it all? How can he possibly learn from anyone of lesser rank? By the way, when was the last time you saw some high-ranking "master" actually do something—that is, aside from taking bows in class? (I'm not talking about those who are in their latter-years and who have already paid their dues; I'm talking about those still young enough to study and train.) It seems that once we take to being called "master," we cease to train because it may prove embarrassingly tough to live up to our inflated credentials.

Case in point

A friend of mine has a small school. A couple of years ago a high-ranking black belt from out of state visited his school and, after watching the class for a while, asked if he could spar. My friend agreed, thinking "What do I have to lose?" If he lost the match, he reasoned, so what; he was only a low-ranking black belt and losing to such a high-ranking instructor is no

FIGURE 12–4   "Whew, this thing's gettin' heavy."

disgrace. On the other hand, if he did well, then so much the better. For him, it really was a win-win situation.

The high-ranking guest's situation was another matter. After he had proudly announced his rank to my friend, his request to spar instantly became, for him, a "no-winner." If he defeated my friend, so what; my friend was only a low-ranking black belt. If, on the other hand, he lost—he would also lose face.

The master did, in fact, lose. During the contest my friend was relaxed and generally having a good time. After the match, his students commented on the visiting "master's" obvious frustration and anger over his inability to best their lowly instructor. It amazes me just how heavy excess baggage can be.

How Much is Pride Worth?

Say what you like, but I respect this "third degree black belt" with the (now) nearly thirty years of martial art experience. He received his rank the hard way—he earned it. He studied under a hard teacher who had high standards, and a third degree black belt from his instructor really means something. This third degree black belt may never get another degree, but he will continue to learn. His rank—or the lack of it—will never be a hindrance to his growth and, as long as he studies, trains, and grows, he will continue to have an art that is alive, vibrant, and of real value—not in terms of dollars perhaps; but in pride.

When I think of masters, a few individuals come to mind. But when they are asked what rank or degree they have, most of them simply reply, "student." Their credentials are often little more than remarks like, "I study with so-and-so right now," (usually someone most of us have never heard of) and "I studied with him (another little known) for so-many years." What should impress us are not ranks and titles, but the fact that real masters are ever students of the art. After decades in the art, these teachers still seek to learn. Teachers like that have no need to proclaim their greatness; their skills do it for them.

Epilogue

A highly respected practitioner and teacher in Denver's martial art community, third degree black belt Hale Hilsabeck is living proof that black belt rank is no indicator of knowledge, skill, or quality of instruction. It may, however, be a far better indicator of character.

THIRTEEN

Quality Instruction—
Where to Find It

You Can Make $100,000 A Year Teaching The Martial Arts!

I know, I do it every year. My name is ——— and I want to show you how you can make money, BIG MONEY, by teaching the martial arts. Exotic cars, beautiful homes, extended vacations and the respect that comes from being financially secure can be yours.

> —Name omitted to protect the
> guilty

In my experience, I have to say that there is a major attitude difference in the openness to new things between instructors with day jobs, and those without. Instructors who make their living teaching martial arts tend to protect their "turf" much more, often claiming the superiority of their systems over the "Brand X" systems. After all, this is how you get market share. Instructors with day jobs teach for the thrill of transmitting information to students and having them learn. It matters a lot less [to them] whether there are 10 or 50 students in the class, as long as those students are there to learn.

> —Daniel Abramovitch
> Martial Art Instructor

The preceding chapter addressed the issue of commercialism and its *"impact on the coveted black belt."* Its conclusion was that too many martial art instructors inflate their credentials to maintain or increase market share. The end result of their actions is a cheapening of the value and real meaning behind "black belt" rank. Certain instructor ranks from among "commercial" martial art schools are reported in that chapter because, being published in the Yellow Pages, those ranks are readily available. In truth, there are many other instructors who are not listed in the Yellow Pages who make equally outlandish claims. Some of them teach on college campuses, others in recreation centers, and a few offer their services to various law enforcement agencies. I can't say there are more good guys out there than scoundrels, but I can say there are many talented, highly skilled and qualified instructors operating and teaching in reputable schools. The trick is finding them.

My purpose in this chapter is to cut through the mystery, marketing hype, and sometimes misguided consumer advisors, to help you be a savvy martial art shopper. Let's begin with this chapter's two opening quotations.

Given a choice between the two, which school would you choose to train in: the one whose instructor seeks to make $100,000 per year, or the one who works a "day job" and teaches simply "for the thrill of transmitting information to students and having them learn?" I know what my initial reaction would be. However, anyone seeking good martial art instruction must, first of all, recognize that "commercial" does not automatically mean *bad*; neither does the "not-for-profit" label necessarily mean *good*. Many other factors figure into the complex equation used to find the right martial art school, including school size, organizational affiliation, international certification, tuition (high and low), and teacher motivation to name just a few. But before we tackle those factors, let's look briefly at martial art consumer guides.

Questions Consumers Should Ask

Every year, numerous articles are published on "How to select a martial art school." Many metropolitan Yellow Pages even provide a telephone number that you can call for suggestions about how to choose a martial art club. Surprisingly, the recorded advise I heard when I called the public service number was not too bad. However, too many of the other published "helpful hints" are often as misguided as they are helpful. For example, an article entitled, "Do your homework on martial arts schools" suggested that prospective consumers ask if the instructor studied with a Japanese master. Also deemed important in this article was knowing if the school is owned by a national chain or an individual. On the surface, such questions seem reasonable, but each displays a lack of knowledge on the writer's part or a bias on the part of the writer's sources.

Assuming that the writer's source in this case did not deliberately exclude Korean, Chinese, Filipino, and other martial arts when he suggested finding out if the instructor had "studied with a Japanese master," the question still implies that Asian instruction, or at least direct lineage to Asian masters, is necessary if you expect to receive authentic martial art training. If you study an art for some cultural benefit, then yes, direct Asian lineage is important, but beyond this it offers no guarantee of training quality or effectiveness.

If the writer's second question referred to some kind of *financial* association with a national organization or franchise, then understand that in the martial arts, franchises and other financial arrangements are *no guarantee* that the school (and the instructor you sign up with) will even be around by this time next year. Likewise, professional affiliation with national or international certification boards are no guarantee that your son or daughter is receiving the best possible instruction. The idea that you should carefully check out a school and its instructor before enrolling is correct, but some of the questions these shoppers' guides suggest completely miss the mark when it comes to martial arts.

Visitors Welcome?

At the very top of any list of questions you have for a school owner should be, "Can I watch the classes?" I'm not just talking about parents observing their children's group classes and private lessons; I mean, are visitors welcome to observe all group classes—even before they enroll their children or themselves? For example, schools that close their doors to visitors because they teach "secret" or "deadly" stuff should be avoided at all costs. The words "secret" and "deadly" should raise large red flags and sound alarms.[1] First of all, you can't teach "secret" stuff and have it remain *secret* for very long—not if it's any good. Second, every reputable instructor I know—including Asian and American teachers of Korean, Japanese, Chinese, and Filipino arts—allows their visitors to observe *all* their group classes. Either a teacher's skills (as reflected in his classes) are up to public scrutiny, or they are not. If a school does not permit visitors—for any reason—scratch it from your list immediately and move on to the next school.[2]

School Size: Bigger or Smaller?

Contrary to popular thinking, large schools[3] are not necessarily bad. For example, a large enrollment means plenty of training partners. Whether you are training for sport or self-defense, a large number (and variety) of training partners is a definite plus. Moreover, schools that maintain large student bodies might be very good places to train. Any school that maintains a large enrollment through word of mouth (that is, without spending a lot on promotional marketing) is, at least, doing a good job of satisfying its customers.

Smaller schools, on the other hand, have their own advantages. Offsetting their disadvantage of fewer training partners is the benefit of a much lower student-to-teacher ratio. Whether in a neighborhood club, semiprivate studio, small school setting, or "backyard dojo," having the opportunity to work with the chief instructor is hard to beat. My last teacher, for example, taught out of his backyard for most of his teaching career, and despite the often less-than-desirable training conditions (like rolling around in dirt dotted with occasional cat droppings and other unpleasantries), the instruction there was exceptional. Some may frown on this kind of training environment, but you must remember that Bruce Lee frequently taught out of his home. Thinking that bigger is better may just cost you the opportunity to train with the likes of a modern day Bruce Lee. Traditionally speaking, small schools and backyard dojos have been very much the norm throughout the East.

All of this is not to say that bigger or smaller is better; both have advantages and disadvantages. Simply use these points and counterpoints when size becomes a factor in evaluating a school.

Organizational Affiliation

National and international affiliation means many things. Primarily it means that teachers and students from the same organization, regardless of geographical location, share common standards and requirements for training, promotion, and rank. A student may move to another city and step into a new school that is in the same organization without so much as skipping a beat. International affiliation can elevate this ability to train anywhere one more notch. A common vocabulary, for example, allows an American Japan Karate Association (JKA) student to train in another JKA school in France, even without knowing French. This is because all of the formal commands are in Japanese. However, large organizations, like large ships at sea, are slow to come about in response to change. For example, if the chief instructor of a large organization discovers that Brazilian jiu-jitsu is effective in self-defense, it remains exceedingly difficult for him to introduce it into the organization's curriculum. This is because the new material has to be taught to all of the instructors in all of the association's schools; new "standard" materials must also be established. Not so with local, unaffiliated schools. New techniques and training methods are much more easily incorporated there.

Without a doubt, students from unaffiliated schools have a more difficult time transferring to other schools because their rank may not be recognized by the receiving instructor or organization. (This is not as much of a problem in black belt ranks as it is among underbelts. Black belt skill is quickly evident, and, once recognized, black belts are often extended the privilege of wearing their hard-earned belts in class—even in a school that is part of another organization.) Despite these difficulties, unaffiliated schools continue to thrive, even without benefit of national or international affiliation. This is because more and more practitioners recognize that comparing ranks between organizations is like comparing apples and oranges. Moreover, most of those joining local, unaffiliated schools are less concerned with rank and international certification than they are with content. Since unaffiliated schools are less interested in maintaining tradition, they usually have broader, more flexible training programs that easily incorporate changes and new ideas. This is often a good fit for the martial art student seeking instruction in self-defense.

Tuition, et al.

According to one article, tuition ranges from $60 to a whopping $130 per month. Some not-for-profit schools offer instruction for as little as $40 per month. But tuition is not the only cost. There may be initiation and testing fees. Find out if there are other fees, and how much they run. This is important because belt-testing fees, for example, can mount—especially if there are a lot of belts between white and black and if the fees increase as the rank being tested moves higher. Also, how often are the students tested and must you pay for a retest? What may start out as $45 a month may end up averaging $60 or more when all of the other fees are added in.

In some schools, tournament competition is a requirement for advancement. Some of the events are intraschool competitions, where the students compete against the same classmates they train with every week. You need to find out how often these events are held, and how much is the entry fee? (Required attendance every two months, at $15 a tournament, increases your monthly cost by $7.50.) Also, find out if you are required to break boards or bricks at tournament (or belt testings for that matter). Do you have to buy your own boards? Beyond the financial pressure, anyone making his living with his hands—like a dentist—might find "breaking" an unacceptable risk to his livelihood. It is important for anyone in a similar situation to find out how passing on the "breaking" requirement might affect promotions.

Contracts

Contracts are common in many commercial martial art schools. But don't let a contract turn you off immediately. We forget that our tuition or monthly dues pay for more than just the instruction we receive. Tuition also pays for the facilities we enjoy. Much like health club agreements, martial art contracts smooth out what would otherwise be a roller-coaster cash flow. Constant cash flow means that when you return from your nice two-week vacation, you still have a heated (or air-conditioned) school in which to train—the summer slump does not drive your favorite instructor out of business.

Other schools avoid contracts, but offer the individual an incentive to pay for three months, six months, or a year in advance. Even those schools that push contracts usually accept students who pay only monthly. You may pay a little more per month, but at least you are not hooked into a contract. If, on the other hand, you don't mind a contract, then remember that a contract of six months to a year is a reasonable term. It benefits both you and the school. The owner gets a smooth cash flow, and you are not unduly committed. This is important because many things can happen in a year: the school can go out of business, you might be transferred out of town, or your priorities may change (marriage and children have a way of changing a lot of things).

Before signing any contract, have an attorney look it over. Have him write in a provision for suspension or complete termination in case of injury (training accident, automobile accident, and so on) or a change in the school's location or ownership. In the case of injury, the school or financial institution may want a written physician's statement, and this is reasonable; just make sure

FIGURE 13–1

that it is *your* physician who makes the determination of your fitness to continue. Any school that objects to these basic protections is one that you probably want to avoid. These are just some of the legal issues to consider before signing any health-industry-related contract. Still, contracts need not be an instant turn-off. You simply need to check them out carefully. That said—paying up front or paying in installments—any instruction costing $130 a month had better be beyond exceptional (or include a lot of private lessons).

Public openness, school size, organizational affiliation, commercial versus not-for-profit, tuition, and contracts—all of these are factors that you must weigh carefully when selecting a place to study and train. But a bigger indicator of instruction quality is teacher motivation. Why does this individual have a martial art school?

Teacher Motivation

There are many reasons for choosing to own and operate a martial art school. Some do it because they love it and want to make a living doing what they enjoy. Apparently there are others who believe that it is one way to make a million bucks (if the advertisement is true, then this is possible in just ten years—at $100,000 per year). There are, of course, those who wish to impress others with their skill and physical prowess (real or imagined). Some do it for social good: they have martial art schools to have a positive impact on the lives they touch. Finally, there is the guy who admits that he opened his school because he doesn't know anything else—fair enough.

Some of the reasons given for having a martial art school sound good; others, perhaps, not so good. However, even the ones we think are questionable may not be as bad as they first sound. Take the fellow who opens a school because he wants to make a living doing what he really enjoys. This is a perfectly legitimate reason for having a school. Everyone should be so fortunate as to make a living doing what he or she loves.

Then there is the instructor who says he teaches martial arts because he doesn't know anything else. This too is an acceptable reason. We should all endeavor to excel in the those areas where we have natural talents and strengths. This kind of reason is not an admission of the lack of skill in other areas; rather, it is a realistic perception of one's strengths. This individual says, "Of all the things I can do, I do this the best. And in this I have the most confidence in my ability to provide for myself and my family." Sounds reasonable to me.

FIGURE 13–2

Let's face it, the most disparaging remarks are inevitably reserved for those who are "out to make a million bucks." We've all seen them: instructors who have the marketing savvy to successfully operate the largest chain of schools in town. Ever notice how these guys are always the targets of most of the other (smaller) school owners? Admittedly, on the surface this "earn a million bucks" motivation seems somehow beneath the ethereal standards of the art, but is it really? Who says that a karate school owner shouldn't be rich, that he should be pennyless and always scraping to make ends meet? In the martial art business very few become wealthy, but what's wrong with wanting to be? And, what of the handful who do make it? Can anyone fault Chuck Norris, Steven Seagal, or Jean Claude VanDamme for parlaying their martial art expertise into financial success? Martial artists need not have the selfless motives of a cloistered monk to be good martial art teachers.

We don't often think of it (probably because we're all guilty of it to varying degrees), but what of the individual whose primary motivation for having a martial art school is impressing others with his skill and physical prowess? Granted, such a motivation *may* make a man a poor teacher, but it has an equal chance of making him a good one. Striving to impress others might compel him to work hard enough to actually be that good. Like we say in the marines, "We don't have an attitude; we're just that good." Working hard and long to be the best might, over time, effect a change of heart. Eventually, as the individual's skill increases he might also experi-

FIGURE 13–3 "That's right, I'm great."

FIGURE 13–4

ence a proportionate decrease in ego (one of the positive benefits of martial art training). Think of the impact such an individual can have on others if his martial art training works this kind of change in his life!

Finally, we come to the individual who has what many see as the purest and highest motivation of all: namely, owning your own school so that you can have a positive impact on the lives you touch. This is truly a noble reason, and there really are teachers so motivated. Many start schools in rough ghetto neighborhoods because they are intimately familiar with what it's like to grow up in such environments. More important, they are equally aware of the kind of positive impact that disciplined and dedicated martial art training can have in helping kids overcome the many disadvantages associated with growing up in ghettos. We often find such individuals serving in the Peace Corps or teaching in the public schools for the same reason. But is even this noble motivation a guarantee that you will receive quality instruction? On the other hand, does a "poor" motivation or reason for being a teacher and operator of a martial art school mean that the instruction you receive there will be equally lacking?

The best way for me to field these questions is to recount my motivation for having a martial art school (my reason for owning and operating a school is not one of those listed above). I have a martial art school because I love teaching: computers, martial arts, whatever—it makes no difference. Nothing fires me up more than teaching something I am interested in to people I care about. But I also have a school so that I can study and train the way I want to—so that I can work on those things that, quite honestly, I need and like. As noble as the first motivation sounds (teaching because I love it), the second (so that I can train the way I want) sounds pretty selfish, huh? While I'm at it, it would be nice to make a $100,000 a year doing this as well. Oh yes, and I do enjoy impressing people with my skill and physical prowess (admittedly, they are not perfect, but I enjoy it nevertheless). And, believe it or not, deep down inside there is a part of me that likes to see my instruction as having a strong positive impact on those who pass through our doors.

About the only reason I left out was *teaching because I know little else.* Sorry, but I have a profession that I thoroughly enjoy. (Actually, I lead sort of a Clark Kent/Superman-type existence: mild mannered computer nerd by day, and martial art teacher by night.) I guess all of this makes my motivation seem more selfish than

FIGURE 13–5   Mild-mannered computer nerd transforms each night into "Karate Man."

noble. But does it? Do I shortchange my students because I teach, primarily, as I wish to train? Do they receive poorer instruction because my motives are not those of a religious monk? The answer to both questions is no.

Whether we admit it or not, most of us open schools so we can train and study as we wish. Martial artists are a strange lot, and it is amazing what we will do to continue our training. What we must remember is that few of us train the same way. Some, for example, prefer full-contact training, and their schools usually emphasize that. Others favor point competition and focus their efforts there. Still others are interested in the traditional, cultural, or health aspects of the art. We have so many different schools with such broad diversity primarily because of the owners' training motivation and personal goals.

Quality From Many Sources

The motivations for owning and operating a martial art school are numerous, and all of them have their merits and detractions. Are there good and bad motives? You bet. Do motives determine the quality of instruction one can expect to receive? To some degree, yes, but the real determining factor is still the instructor's ability to teach you what you want to learn.

When evaluating a martial art by its technical capabilities, skills, and potential, it is important that you find out what the school teaches and what the teacher's philosophy of training is. Ask, "What do you teach (striking, grappling, both) and why? Do you emphasize self-defense, sport karate, low or high kicking?" If you have a bad back or problem knees, find out what percentage of their training consists of hand techniques as opposed to kicking techniques? Then, and only then, do you tell them what *you* are looking for. (There are, unfortunately, those who will promise you anything, so that they can take you for everything while giving you nothing.)

The instructor's motivation for having a school is important, but even this is not as important as his character and teaching ability. Even seemingly questionable motivation for operating a martial art school can still result in quality instruction if it is coupled with *integrity* and *good teaching skills.* For myself, I confess, I have a martial art school so that I can train the way I wish. I teach, however, for a different reason. I teach because I love it and I'm good at. And for me, those are the best reasons of all.

Conclusion

Compared to Asia's martial art legacy, American experience in the arts is undeniably short. However, our short duration in the arts is offset by the unprecedented breadth of knowledge that is available to us. For scores of years now, Americans have had access to the widest possible range of Asian martial arts: Chinese, Japanese, Korean, Filipino, Indonesian and many others. This access, coupled with our freedom to choose and study one or more arts, reduces considerably any disparity between Eastern and Western martial art knowledge and experience. We know enough now to question the status quo.

Despite our breadth of experience in Eastern arts, only a handful of American practitioners have seriously challenged the classical practices addressed here. Those who tried often found themselves ostracized by the rest of the established martial art community. (Bruce Lee is an excellent example of this.) Even some of the more "progressive" martial artists today still cling to some very classical but outdated customs.

What is advocated here is not the elimination of all cultural, classical, or traditional practices from the martial arts. Exploring a rich cultural treasure is very rewarding and, for some, the strongest motivator to study and train. And who can argue against teaching self-discipline, courtesy, respect for others, and how to focus your energies on a given task or goal? All of these are part of classical martial arts. However, other changes are still warranted, and some of them are long overdue. Training in shoes, updating punching and blocking methods, and using the national or common tongue are just three examples of the kind of change that is needed.

Obviously, there are exceptions. Where the common or national tongue cannot provide an accurate translation of a term or technique, then use the language that will. The word *chi* is a good example. *Synergy* is the closest English word that fully and concisely captures the indescribable essence of *chi*. Still, within our community, synergy may be too obscure a term to catch on quickly. It makes sense then, to use Eastern terms in cases like this, until better ones are found and become commonly recognized and accepted substitutes.

Other exceptions are just common sense. Where a single strong-arm classical block is the best move for a particular technique or a situation, use it. If some ancient herbal liniment relieves the pain and promotes healing of a training injury, then by all means apply it. If a school has invested thousands of dollars to provide a mat for the students' safety, then don't ruin it by wearing shoes on it. But also use common sense in avoiding training methods and practices that are counterproductive.

Sharing Cultural Traditions

America is a cultural melting pot. If your heritage is Asian, African, or European, and the art you study is from your ancestral homeland, great. Cultural pursuits bring purpose, pride, and fulfillment to our lives. If you are an instructor, just do a favor for those who do not share your cultural roots: tell them that cultural preservation is one of your training goals. Let them decide if your goals are compatible with theirs. If it turns out that they are, great. But if it happens that your students are not particularly interested in preserving another heritage, but you accept them as students nonetheless, then make sure that you do not penalize them—either by holding them back or by advancing only those who share your feelings—simply because they do not share your purpose. I know a very knowledgeable and highly skilled Filipino instructor who tells everyone up front that his purpose is to preserve the memory of his teacher and his cultural heritage through his sharing of the art. I respect that. I disagree with what he seeks to preserve and some of his reasons supporting his position; however I respect his honesty.

Some Problems of Our Own

For our part, honesty demands the admission that not all of the problems plaguing martial arts in America are Asian in origin. As discount karate schools pump out more and more "cardboard" black belts—black belts on paper only, possessing nothing near "black belt" skill—respect for the coveted belt erodes. Is it any wonder that instructors (Asian and American) inflate their credentials with such predictable regularity? The American martial art garden is, indeed, overgrown, and in desperate need of weeding. *Martially* speaking, we inherited a slough of Asian weeds. However, instead of pulling those weeds, we planted a few of our own. I think the imported ones will be a good deal easier to remove than our own home-grown variety.

A Personal Note

Many fine martial artists have influenced my attitudes and the path my study has taken. A number of them I know only from their writings. Although I quote Ed Parker frequently, my knowledge of him and his insights comes largely from his published works. I was, however, fortunate enough to have personal contact with him on two occasions: the first was at a black belt seminar he was presenting, and the second was a personal long-distance telephone conversation. Allow me to conclude by sharing these experiences.

A few years before he passed away, I was invited to an Ed Parker seminar by one of his black belts. I was a few minutes late arriving, and the seminar had already begun. On entering the training area, I was promptly and politely asked to leave because the seminar was open only to Parker black belts. Before the gentleman who invited me could speak up, Mr. Parker said, "No, let him stay." I have never been a student of Ed Parker, but rarely have I felt more welcome at any martial art event than I did that day.

During the seminar Mr. Parker asked if anyone knew the technique where someone grabs your wrist and you bring your assailant to his knees by pinning his fingers to your wrist and rotating your hand over his wrist. No one answered, so I raised my hand. Mr. Parker was only about three feet from me, and, as quick as a flash, he grabbed my wrist and said, "Good. Do it." Without a second's hesitation I clamped on to his hand and brought him convincingly to his knees. (I was not about to insult this man by treating him as anything less than what he really was—a martial art master.) Every black belt in the place (we were all in a line) leaned forward with a look of shock. On seeing their faces I just knew I was dead. I could see it: *death at the hands of twenty black belts.* Instead, the ever-gracious Ed Parker

Author with Ed Parker at the seminar.

looked up and with an approving grin said, "Good job. Now, let's see . . ." I can't remember what he said after that; I was too busy thanking God for sparing my miserable life.

Frankly, I don't remember a single technique from that afternoon session. Nor do I recall seeing Parker's blinding speed or some fascinating movement. I am sure both were there in abundance, I simply cannot recall them. However, one thing I will never forget was his approving grin—the man actually enjoyed the contact. Ed Parker was a real martial artist and a true master of his art.

My second contact with Ed Parker was a telephone conversation. Sometime after the seminar, I asked the black belt who had invited me if he would inquire of Mr. Parker to see if he would consider reviewing a notebook/workbook that I had compiled for my students. (That notebook eventually formed the basis of this work.) To my surprise, Mr. Parker agreed and my friend forwarded the work to him. (Remember, Parker was doing this for someone outside of his organization, someone completely unaffiliated with him.)

About three months later I received a phone call. To my surprise, it was Ed Parker! He remembered me and he said something that I will never forget. After making a couple of historical corrections, he said that it was good to see someone else travel a similar but different path and come to many of the same conclusions that he had. We spoke for only fifteen minutes or so, but I was greatly encouraged by his words. Since then I've read everything he has published. Parker's logical approach to martial arts and his true humility are a constant inspiration to me. It seems fitting then, that I close with the following quotation from him (Parker 1982, 121):

> Seek martial arts knowledge with utmost scrutiny. *Do not become entranced by impractical or useless movements.* Above all, do not be categorized as one who "Learns more and more about less and less until he ends up learning everything there is to know about nothing" [emphasis added].

If William Shakespeare were alive in our day, he would, doubtless, use a personal computer with a modern word processor to write his plays. His genius would still produce classical works, but his material would be contemporary, his language would be modern English, and his methods suited to the day. Shouldn't we do likewise?

Notes

Chapter Two

1. *Shearing* is the application of opposing forces along parallel lines. For an in-depth study and explanation of this principle, see *Indonesian Fighting Fundamentals*, Paladin Press, 1996.
2. It goes without saying that the availability and use of firearms played a large part in rendering such fighting skills as swordsmanship and archery ineffective for self-defense, but equally important was the conscious shift away from self-defense training in favor of self-development and perfection of character.

Chapter Three

1. Yip Man (?–1972) was grandmaster of the wing chun style of kung fu.

Chapter Four

1. Outside this chapter and throughout the remainder of this book, "combat" means actual, self-defense, *street* application; not military application.

Chapter Five

1. These papers are not graded, critiqued, or evaluated on grammar or literary skill; not everyone has equal writing abilities. What we look for is content.
2. Accelerator, clutch, brake, turn indicator, steering wheel, and gearshift.

Chapter Six

1. "Cracking the turtle's shell" is an expression that refers to the ability to smash through samurai armor.

2. In fairness, both arts prefer avoidance and evasion over blocking.
3. By "limited," I mean that boxers cannot use the full array of hand weapons available to the Asian martial artist (i.e. elbows, forearms, and hands).
4. For lack of a better term, I will use the word, "multihand," to distinguish this method from its classical counterpart—primarily, the single strong-arm block.
5. A *makiwara* is a bundle of straw used as a target. Often this is affixed to a post or wall and covered with rope or canvas.
6. The movement, is called "block-right" because it blocks the attacking arm *to the right*. It matters not whether the attack is a right or left punch; the movement works the same for either.
7. Block-left, is not, for us, a mirror image of block-right. In block-left, the defender's right hand intercepts his opponent's punch nearer the attacker's elbow than his hand. The defender's left hand, chambered at his right shoulder, follows his right and displaces it at the opponent's elbow. This asymmetrical approach is explained in detail in my other book, *Indonesian Fighting Fundamentals,* published by Paladin Press, 1996.
8. Commercially available mats that better handle training in shoes are making an appearance. They are expensive, though. Currently, the mid-price is about $30 a square yard.

Chapter Seven

1. To prevent the terms *form, forms,* and *forms training* from becoming tedious, I will also use the Japanese term kata to describe this training method, since kata is a term that is generally recognized among Western martial art practitioners.
2. Far too many competitors today (especially younger competitors) work harder on their style, "attitude," and acrobatics, than they do on understanding and application of the martial techniques they perform. Some argue that this is actually good. They reason that, as instructors, they would not want their young charges to be in full possession of the real potential behind what they do. However, this kind of logic fails because the student never develops a healthy respect for what he has and its fearsome potential—much like playing with toy guns.

Chapter Eight

1. Although not the most accurate term, "sport karate," is universally recognized as encompassing the sporting and competitive element of Asian martial arts.
2. Saying that this event was the "first large-scale karate tournament" does not mean that it was the first tournament or competitive martial event; it was not.

It was, however, the one that led the way for the kinds of modern sport karate competition so popular today.

3. I cannot recall who first used it, but the water polo/lifesaving analogy is from a quotation lamenting that "Those who scramble to frantically 'legitimatize' karate (the art) into a sporting (even Olympic) event might see water polo as the legitimate representation of lifesaving."

Chapter Nine

1. Feminine participation in martial sports, like the Chinese wushu teams, is considerable, and has been so for many years. However, this discussion is limited to martial *arts* only—specifically excluding martial sports.
2. By definition, bravado is: *a pretentious, swaggering display of courage.*
3. Groin protection has been available for more than thirty years. Really good protection has been available for the last five. The myths that groin protection gives one a false sense of security, or that the protection is insufficient, are not true. Unless one is kicking to the head, the groin is more difficult to hit and better protected than even one's face. Moreover, during nearly thirty years of training with groin protection, I have never gotten used to being hit there.

Chapter Ten

1. This example is, admittedly, oversimplified because every item in this list is not of equal value. However, for the purposes here, this linear approach is useful for explaining synergy and its effect.

Chapter Eleven

1. I am referring to those who follow historical Islam, Judaism, and Christianity—those faiths that are practiced as taught in their scriptures—and not, for example, someone whose view of Judaism or Christianity is that of one who has not embraced the Bible.
2. In English, these expressions are rendered: straddle stance or horse stance, front kick, and forefist middle inside block and lower parry.

Chapter Twelve

1. According to the 1995 American Heritage Dictionary, the first definition of a "black belt" is "the rank of *expert* in a martial art such as judo or karate" [emphasis added].
2. The inability to meet basic physical requirements also prevents many from becoming police officers, fire fighters, and members of the armed forces.

Chapter Thirteen

1. The place for lethal techniques in the artial artist's arsenal is addressed in Chapter Four.
2. Obviously, disruptive visitors are never welcome.
3. A *large school* is very different from a *large class*. A large school may have many students, but with class sizes that are considerably smaller. Although "large" is a relative term, 100 students in a class is too big by any scale. However, recommending a standard teacher-to-student ratio is difficult because the ratio varies widely depending on such factors as the material being presented, the skill level of the participants, and the instructor's ability to communicate what he is teaching.

References

Advertisements. (1996, May). *Black Belt.* pp. 70, 142.

Beaver, William K. (1992, April). George Anderson—Karate's Renaissance Man. *Karate Kung-fu Illustrated.*

Breen, Andrew (quoting Stephen K. Hayes). (1995, October). The Kicks of Ninjutsu. *Black Belt.*

Clark, Rick. (1989, June). What is the Purpose of Kata. *Inside Karate.* p. 61.

Dickens, Dennis. (1993, October). Letters: "Finding the Truth." *Inside Kung-Fu.* p.127.

Funakoshi, Gichin. (1981). Karate-do: My Way of Life. Tokyo, New York, London: Kodansha, International.

Glass, W. Bentley. (1993, February). Letters. *Inside Kung-Fu.*

Gleeson, Geoff. R. (1967). *Judo for the West.* South Brunswick and New York: A. S. Barnes and Company. p. 13.

Liszewski, Steve. (1995, November). "ClassAct," *The Client/Server Observer.* p. 2.

Long, Kathy. (1992, May). Letters. *Black Belt.* p. 8.

Lowry, Dave. (1987, June). Anachronisms, "Shikijima Do: The Japanese Way." *Inside Karate.*

Lowry, Dave. (1992, November). The Value of Blocking. *Black Belt.*

Lowry, Dave. (1993, November). The Perfect Training Surface. *Black Belt.*

Maliszewski, Michael. (1992, July). "Fighting Arts and Martial Ways," *Journal of Asian Martial Arts.* Vol.1, No. 3.

Parker, Ed. (1982). *Infinite Insights into Kenpo: Mental Stimulation.* Vol. 1, 1982. Los Angeles: Delsby Publications.

Random, Michael. (1985). The Martial Arts. *Swordsmanship, Kendo, Aikido, Judo, Karate.* London: Peerage Books.

Scientific Premium Company, USA. (1992, December). "CHI: The Power of Two Galaxies," *Inside Kung-Fu.*

Sigman, Mike: "On Qi and Qigong Exercises," *Tai Chi* magazine, Vol. 16, No. 6. December, 1992.

Sturman, Mike. (1995, October). The System: Brutal Russian Martial Art Resembles Bruce Lee's Jeet Kune Do. *Black Belt.* p. 31.

Thomas, Chris. (1993, April). The Strange Evolution of Goju-ryu Karate Kata. *Black Belt.*

Wallace, Bill. (1992, March). Front Kicks, "Kickboxing: It's a Man's World." *Black Belt.*

Webster's New Collegiate Dictionary. (1979).

About the Author

A computer professional for more than thirty years, Bob Orlando was introduced to the martial arts while on active duty in the United States Marines (1961–1964). However, it was not until after he left the service that this flicker of interest kindled there became his consuming fire. Bob began serious study in Chinese kenpo-karate. Later he switched to kung fu, studying under Al Dacascos (then teaching in Denver, Colorado). His training with Dacascos lasted three years until a back operation made it impossible to continue in Dacascos' high-kicking style of kung fu. It was back to Chinese kenpo, where Bob received his first degree black-belt from Dr. John P.Cochran. Although he has subsequently earned additional rank, he prefers to say that he is a student of the art and leave it at that. "Rank" he says, "is excess baggage. It becomes a hindrance to learning because everyone expects that you already know everything."

Ever a student of the arts, Bob's quest for knowledge has taken him into aikido, iaido, arnis de mano, and eskrima. However, what has impacted him the most are the years he has spent studying Chinese kuntao and Indonesian pentjak silat under Dutch-Indonesian master Willem de Thouars.

A graduate of a Jesuit university, Bob is the author of *Indonesian Fighting Fundamentals: The Brutal Arts of the Archipelago,* and has written numerous articles for both national and local publication. No longer a tournament competitor, Bob still supports tournament karate and is a founding member and director of the Colorado Karate Association—a nonprofit organization that works to provide competitors with a positive tournament environment.

Although he is not a "professional" martial artist (one who makes his living from martial arts), Bob still considers himself a "full-time" martial artist, for he studies and trains constantly. Of his own abilities, he says, "I have many skills, but not because I have any natural talent; I've simply worked very hard to get to where I am today. My fortés are my analytical mind and my ability to share what I know with others. I take the complicated and make it simple. I am a teacher."

Sola Deo Gloria